HOW TO START AND FINISH STRONG

COLLEGE PREP

VOLUME 2

I0140857

KEY STRATEGIES FOR SPIRITUAL GROWTH

"For no one can lay any other foundation than what has been laid down. That foundation is Jesus Christ." - 1 Corinthians 3:11 CSB

Jesus said, "I will show you what someone is like who comes to me, hears my words, and acts on them: "He is like a man building a house, who dug deep and laid the foundation on the rock. When the flood came, the river crashed against that house and couldn't shake it, because it was well built." - Luke 6:47-48 CSB

With deep appreciation to my wife Diane for her support and dedicated to our grandsons Graham and Peter that they may build their lives on a solid spiritual foundation.

Note: The series *How to Start and Finish Strong* has two volumes:

College Prep Volume 1 – A Mostly Scripture Approach
College Prep Volume 2 – Key Strategies for Spiritual Growth

There are corresponding eBook versions with all Bible verses fully expanded. The Appendix is the same in both Volumes.

HOW TO START AND FINISH STRONG

COLLEGE PREP

VOLUME 2

KEY STRATEGIES FOR SPIRITUAL GROWTH

*A*dvantage
BOOKS

THOMAS WITZIG

College Prep Volume 2 – Key Strategies for Spiritual Growth by Thomas Witzig

Copyright © 2024 by Thomas Witzig

All Rights Reserved.

ISBN: 978-1-59755-790-0

Published by: ADVANTAGE BOOKS™, Longwood, FL. www.advbookstore.com

Library of Congress Catalog Number: 2024937467	
Name:	Witzig, Thomas Author
Title:	*College Prep – Key Strategies for Spiritual Growth*
	Thomas Witzig
	Advantage Books, 2024
Identifiers:	ISBN Paperback: 9781597557900
	ISBN eBook: 9781597558013
Subjects:	RELIGION: Christian Life – Inspirational RELIGION:
	Christian Life – Spiritual Growth

First Printing: November 2024

24 25 26 27 28 29 30   10 9 8 7 6 5 4 3 2 1

Table of Contents

Foreword

In Volume 1 "College Prep – A Mostly Scripture Approach" the focus was establishing your spiritual foundation on Biblical truth and understanding how Genesis 1-11 is so relevant to the current issues of today. If for some reason you did not read Volume 1, I would encourage you to do so since it's difficult to build your spiritual life without a solid foundation of Biblical truth. Volume 2 describes through Scripture and discussion questions how to face key personal issues that you will encounter as you journey through life (**Figure 1**).

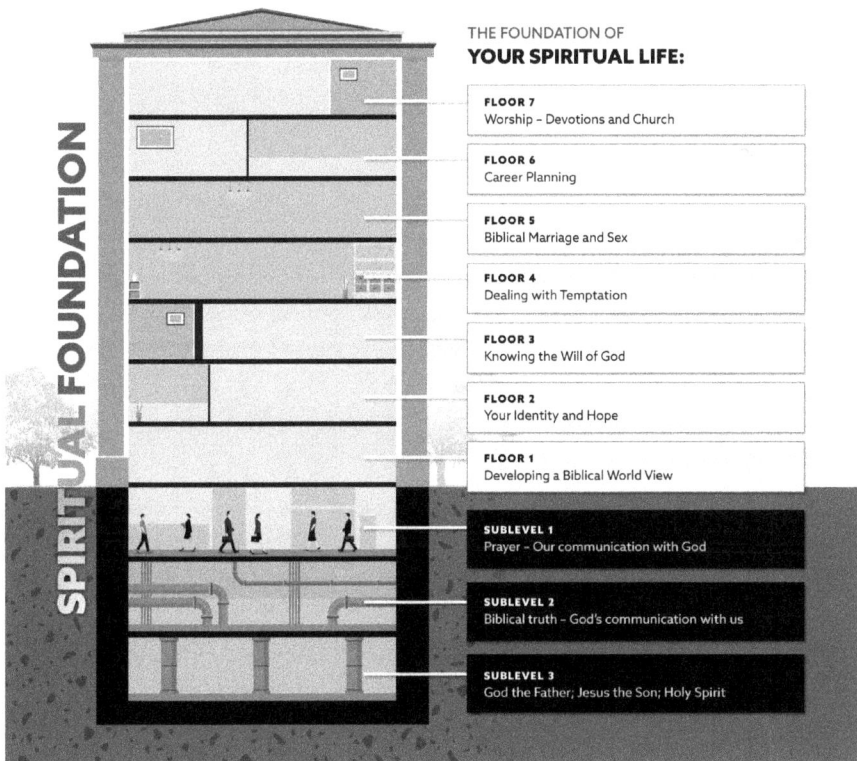

THE FOUNDATION OF
YOUR SPIRITUAL LIFE:

FLOOR 7
Worship – Devotions and Church

FLOOR 6
Career Planning

FLOOR 5
Biblical Marriage and Sex

FLOOR 4
Dealing with Temptation

FLOOR 3
Knowing the Will of God

FLOOR 2
Your Identity and Hope

FLOOR 1
Developing a Biblical World View

SUBLEVEL 1
Prayer – Our communication with God

SUBLEVEL 2
Biblical truth – God's communication with us

SUBLEVEL 3
God the Father; Jesus the Son; Holy Spirit

SPIRITUAL FOUNDATION

Figure 1: The key issues that will impact your life and determine how you run the spiritual race set out for you.

In this book the Bible is the main text and all the important topics such as marriage and sex will be supported with Biblical truth. You, the reader, should want to know what

God says about these topics not just some other human's opinion. The Bible is the authority in all matters and God knows best how to handle these issues since He was your designer and creator. In addition to the verses that are quoted, the bolded sentences highlight the nuggets of truth contained in the Bible passages. The questions in each section aim to get you to apply the concepts to your own life and guide your discussion with others if you are in a small group. *Do not avoid these as they are meant to show current examples of real-world issues that are addressed in the Bible.* Lastly, read the Appendix now if you are uncertain about your relationship with Jesus Christ.

1

Who Am I? Why Am I here?
Does Anybody Love Me?
What is My Hope?

This chapter builds on a Biblical foundation and uses the Bible to address key issues and situations that you will encounter as you journey through life. It begins with the important concept of knowing who you are in God's eyes and what is your ultimate hope and destination. Having a healthy view of oneself (self-esteem) is "really healthy". Self-esteem is not pride; rather, it is realizing our value and worth to God. The world can be a cold and nasty place unless our self-worth is solidly rooted in the Bible promises and concepts of individual worth. The Bible says that each of us was born with a purpose and God knew us *in utero* (when we were still inside our mother). We were and are in God's thoughts and our purpose is to please God. He takes pleasure in us every day. He is our Spiritual Father.

• *Who am I? A creation in the image of God.*
"So God created man in his own image; he created him in the image of God; he created them male and female." - Genesis 1:27 CSB

• *Why am I here? You were created with a purpose; you are not an accident. You are a unique creation and God knew you from the moment of your conception. He thinks about you, is with you and knows everything about you.*
"Listen to me, descendants of Jacob, all you who remain in Israel. I have cared for you since you were born. *Yes, I carried you before you were born*. I will be your God throughout your lifetime--until your hair is white with age. I made you, and I will care for you. I will carry you along and save you." - Isaiah 46:3-4 NLT

Blessed is the God and Father of our Lord Jesus Christ, who has blessed us with every spiritual blessing in the heavens in Christ. *For he chose us in him, before the foundation of the world, to be holy and blameless in love before him.* - Ephesians 1:3-4 CSB

Ishmael, David, Jeremiah, Samson, Jesus, John the Baptist, and Paul were all recognized *in utero* and were created with a purpose.

• *Jesus – these verses from Isaiah 49 are in reference to Jesus.*

"Listen to me, all you in distant lands! Pay attention, you who are far away! The LORD called me before my birth; from within the womb he called me by name. ... And now the LORD speaks--the one who formed me in my mother's womb to be his servant, who commissioned me to bring Israel back to him. The LORD has honored me, and my God has given me strength." - Isaiah 49:1, 5 NLT

• *John the Baptist the forerunner of Jesus; the only person said to have been filled with the Holy Spirit while still in utero.*

"An angel of the Lord appeared to him, standing to the right of the altar of incense. When Zechariah saw him, he was terrified and overcome with fear. But the angel said to him: Do not be afraid, Zechariah, because your prayer has been heard. Your wife Elizabeth will bear you a son, and you will name him John. There will be joy and delight for you, and many will rejoice at his birth. For he will be great in the sight of the Lord and will never drink wine or beer. *He will be filled with the Holy Spirit while still in his mother's womb.* He will turn many of the children of Israel to the Lord their God. And he will go before him in the spirit and power of Elijah, to turn the hearts of fathers to their children, and the disobedient to the understanding of the righteous, to make ready for the Lord a prepared people." - Luke 1:11-17 CSB

• *Ishmael was identified and named before he was born to Hagar.*

"And the angel of the LORD said to her, Behold, you are pregnant and shall bear a son. You shall call his name Ishmael, because the LORD has listened to your affliction." - Genesis 16:11 ESV

• *David – the King of Israel.*

"For it was you who created my inward parts; you knit me together in my mother's womb. I will praise you because *I have been remarkably and wondrously made.* Your works are wondrous, and I know this very well. My bones were not hidden from you when I was made in secret, when I was formed in the depths of the earth. *Your eyes saw me when I was formless; all my days were written in your book and planned before a single one of them began.* God, how precious your thoughts are to me; how vast their sum is! If I counted them, they would outnumber the grains of sand; when I wake up, I am still with you." - Psalm 139:13-18 CSB

• Samson, the judge of Israel was predicted to save the nation of Israel at that time in history.

"For behold, you shall conceive and bear a son. No razor shall come upon his head, for the child shall be a Nazirite to God from the womb, and he shall begin to save Israel from the hand of the Philistines." - Judges 13:5 ESV

• Jeremiah was designed to be a prophet – before he was even born!

"The LORD gave me this message: I knew you before I formed you in your mother's womb. *Before you were born I set you apart and appointed you* as my prophet to the nations." - Jeremiah 1:4-5 NLT

• Paul – chosen before birth – by grace.

"*But even before I was born, God chose me* and called me by his marvelous grace. Then it pleased him" - Galatians 1:15 NLT

All of us were created for God's pleasure; therefore, we each have meaning.

"You are worthy, O Lord our God, to receive glory and honor and power. *For you created all things, and they exist because you created what you pleased.*" - Revelation 4:11 NLT

• God knows us personally – He knows our heart.

"And God, *who knows the heart,* bore witness to them by giving them the Holy Spirit, just as he also did to us." - Acts 15:8 CSB

• God loves us. He loved us so much He sent Jesus to die for us.

"For God loved the world so much that he gave his one and only Son, *so that everyone who believes in him will not perish but have eternal life.*" - John 3:16 NLT

"To all who are in Rome, *loved by God,* called as saints. Grace to you and peace from God our Father and the Lord Jesus Christ." - Romans 1:7 CSB

• *This love of God gives us confidence and quenches our fear. If we love God and understand that He loves us, we will love others and care for them.*

And we have come to know and to *believe the love that God has for us. God is love*, and the one who remains in love remains in God, and God remains in him. In this, love is made complete with us *so that we may have confidence in the day of judgment*, because as he is, so also are we in this world. There is *no fear in love*; instead, perfect love drives out fear, because fear involves punishment. So the one who fears is not complete in love. We love because he first loved us. If anyone says, "I love God," and yet hates his brother or sister, he is a liar. For the person who does not love his brother or sister whom he has seen cannot love God whom he has not seen. And we have this command from him: *The one who loves God must also love his brother and sister.* - 1 John 4:16-21 CSB

How does the Bible refer to us? What does it call us?

If you are a follower of Jesus, you are called a "a child of God". This is an enduring term that encourages us to develop a close relationship through prayer and worship with God our Father. You are also called "God's treasure" which is meant to impress on you how important you are to God. You are also a "saint" and a part of the whole "family of God". Lastly, Christians are called "sheep" and Jesus is our leader, our Shepherd.

• *Children - we are children and God is our Spiritual Father.* We are His children and heirs to eternity where we will be glorified with Him someday. As a child you gain an inheritance from God the Father – that inheritance is eternity in Heaven.

"For all who are led by the Spirit of God are children of God. So you have not received a spirit that makes you fearful slaves. Instead, you received God's Spirit *when he adopted you as his own children.* Now we call him, "Abba, Father." For his Spirit joins with our spirit *to affirm that we are God's children.* And since we are his children, we are his heirs. In fact, together with Christ we are heirs of God's glory. But if we are to share his glory, we must also share his suffering." - Romans 8:14-17 NLT
Romans 8:16-17

• *Called ones - called to serve God.*
"We know that all things work together for the good of those who love God, *who are called according to his purpose.*" - Romans 8:28 CSB

"I pray that the eyes of your heart may be enlightened so that you may know what is the *hope of his calling, what is the wealth of his glorious inheritance in the saints*," - Ephesians 1:18 CSB

• Fellow citizens.
"So then you are no longer foreigners and strangers, *but fellow citizens with the saints*, and members of God's household," - Ephesians 2:19 CSB

• Sons of God.
"Blessed are the peacemakers, for they will be called sons of God." - Matthew 5:9 CSB

"for through faith you are all sons of God in Christ Jesus." - Galatians 3:26 CSB

• Treasured by God. The example of Daniel.
"He gave me this explanation: Daniel, I've come now to give you understanding. At the beginning of your petitions an answer went out, and I have come to give it, *for you are treasured by God*. So consider the message and understand the vision." - Daniel 9:22-23 CSB

• Sheep – the Bible and Jesus use sheep as a metaphor for people. We are the sheep and Jesus is the shepherd. As John 10:6 says this is a figure of speech or a metaphor.
"For you were *like sheep going astray*, but you have now returned to the Shepherd and Overseer of your souls." - 1 Peter 2:25 CSB

"For he is our God, and we are the people of his pasture, *the sheep under his care*. Today, if you hear his voice: " - Psalm 95:7 CSB

"Acknowledge that the LORD is God. He made us, and we are his-- his people, the *sheep of his pasture*." - Psalm 100:3 CSB

"When he saw the crowds, he felt compassion for them, because they were distressed and dejected, *like sheep without a shepherd*." - Matthew 9:36 CSB

"*Jesus gave them this figure of speech*, but they did not understand what he was telling them. ...I am the gate. If anyone enters by me, he will be saved and will come in and go out and find pasture. A thief comes only to steal and kill and destroy. I have come so that they may have life and have it in abundance. *I am the good shepherd. The good shepherd lays down his life for the sheep.* The hired hand, since he is not the shepherd and doesn't own the sheep, leaves them and runs away when he sees a wolf coming. The wolf then snatches and scatters them. This happens because he is a hired hand and doesn't care about the sheep. I am the good shepherd. I know my own, and my own know me, "just as the Father knows me, and I know the Father. *I lay down my life for the sheep.*" - John 10:6, 9-15 CSB

• *Saints – if you are a follower of Jesus, you are called a "saint".*
"To the church of God at Corinth, *to those sanctified in Christ Jesus, called as saints,* with all those in every place who call on the name of Jesus Christ our Lord -- both their Lord and ours." - 1 Corinthians 1:2 CSB

"To all who are in Rome, loved by God, *called as saints.* Grace to you and peace from God our Father and the Lord Jesus Christ." - Romans 1:7 CSB

"In the same way the Spirit also helps us in our weakness, because we do not know what to pray for as we should, but the Spirit himself intercedes for us with unspoken groanings. And he who searches our hearts knows the mind of the Spirit, because he *intercedes for the saints* according to the will of God." - Romans 8:26-27 CSB

God has a plan for your life – it is to serve Him. God has a special life course set specifically for you – run that course and trust God to make it happen.

"Therefore, since we are surrounded by such a huge crowd of witnesses to the life of faith, let us strip off every weight that slows us down, especially the sin that so easily trips us up. *And let us run with endurance the race God has set before us.*" - Hebrews 12:1 NLT

• *God cares for us and will be with us on this journey through life.*
"The LORD replied, "*I will personally go with you, Moses*, and I will give you rest-- everything will be fine for you." - Exodus 33:14 NLT

• *Our job is not to worry about God's plans for others; rather, focus on following Him.*
"When Peter saw him, he said to Jesus, Lord, what about him? If I want him to remain until I come, Jesus answered, what is that to you? As for you, follow me." - John 21:21-22 CSB

We need to show love to God.

• *Loving God is demonstrated by keeping His commandments.*

"*The one who has my commands and keeps them is the one who loves me.* And the one who loves me will be loved by my Father. I also will love him and will reveal myself to him." - John 14:21 CSB

• *We also need to love ourselves enough to care for ourselves and understand our self-worth and self-esteem.*

"The commandments, Do not commit adultery; do not murder; do not steal; do not covet; and any other commandment, are summed up by this commandment: *Love your neighbor as yourself.*" - Romans 13:9 CSB

What is our hope? It is the promise of eternity.

• *We may suffer on earth, but heaven is our hope.* Your ultimate future is bright no matter what is happening to you on earth. Always take the long view so that you can endure the current situation.

"Therefore, brothers and sisters, *be patient until the Lord's coming.* See how the farmer waits for the precious fruit of the earth and is patient with it until it receives the early and the late rains. *You also must be patient. Strengthen your hearts, because the Lord's coming is near.* Brothers and sisters, do not complain about one another, so that you will not be judged. Look, the judge stands at the door! Brothers and sisters, take the prophets who spoke in the Lord's name as *an example of suffering and patience.* See, we count as blessed those who have endured. You have heard of Job's endurance and have seen the outcome that the Lord brought about -- the Lord is compassionate and merciful." - James 5:7-11 CSB

• *Our ultimate hope is in eternity where we will be with Jesus. This is the promise of the resurrection and life eternal with Jesus.*

"Now concerning the resurrection of the dead, haven't you read what was spoken to you by God: I am the God of Abraham and the God of Isaac and the God of Jacob? *He is not the God of the dead, but of the living.*" - Matthew 22:31-32 CSB
2 Corinthians 4:16-18

• *Our hope is living (its real not fake) and it can never die. The hope is in the resurrected Jesus. We do not base hope on someone in the grave.*

"Blessed be the God and Father of our Lord Jesus Christ. Because of his great mercy he has given us new birth *into a living hope through the resurrection of Jesus Christ* from the dead and into an inheritance that is imperishable, undefiled, and unfading, kept in heaven for you." - 1 Peter 1:3-4 CSB

1 Peter 1:8-9

• *We shall see Him face to face.*

"Dear friends, we are God's children now, and what we will be, has not yet been revealed. We know that when he appears, we will be like him because we will see him as he is." - 1 John 3:2 CSB

• *The LORD is our source of strength – we need to trust in that.*

"but those who trust in the LORD will renew their strength; they will soar on wings like eagles; they will run and not become weary, they will walk and not faint." - Isaiah 40:31 CSB

• *Hope is fueled by reading the Bible.*

"For whatever was written in the past was written for our instruction, *so that we may have hope through endurance and through the encouragement from the Scriptures.*" - Romans 15:4 CSB

How can I be happy in this life until I get to Heaven?

• *Jesus said we must hunger for righteousness, and we will be satisfied and happy. The Greek word for "blessed" is makerios which means "happy".*

"Blessed are those who hunger and thirst for righteousness, for they will be filled." - Matthew 5:6 CSB

• *We wait and live holy lives.*

"Since all these things are to be dissolved in this way, *it is clear what sort of people you should be in holy conduct and godliness as you wait for the day of God* and hasten its coming. Because of that day, the heavens will be dissolved with fire and the elements will melt with heat. But based on his promise, *we wait for new heavens and a new earth*, where righteousness dwells. Therefore, *dear friends, while you wait for these things*, make every effort to be found without spot or blemish in his sight, at peace." - 2 Peter 3:11-14 CSB

• *We have a great advantage since we "know with certainty" what our ultimate destination is. We are to "grow in grace and knowledge of Jesus".*

"Therefore, dear friends, *since you know this in advance,* be on your guard, so that you are not led away by the error of lawless people and fall from your own stable position. But grow in the grace and knowledge of our Lord and Savior Jesus Christ. To him be the glory both now and to the day of eternity." - 2 Peter 3:17-18 CSB

• *Our reward is referred to as "crowns" and unlike the rewards of this life they do not fade. The Chief Shepherd refers to Jesus.*

"And when the chief Shepherd appears, you will receive the *unfading crown of glory*." - 1 Peter 5:4 CSB

Despite the above verses why do I still feel lonely?

• *Sometimes we do not feel close to God; it happened to David the Psalmist.*

"O LORD, why do you stand so far away? Why do you hide when I am in trouble?" - Psalm 10:1 NLT

"My eyes are always on the LORD, for he rescues me from the traps of my enemies. Turn to me and have mercy, *for I am alone and in deep distress*. My problems go from bad to worse. Oh, save me from them all!" - Psalm 25:15-17 NLT

• *Loneliness is often accompanied by fear. Remember, God is right there. Nothing can separate us from the love of God – we are inseparable.*

"*Do not fear, for I am with you*; do not be afraid, for I am your God. I will strengthen you; I will help you; I will hold on to you with my righteous right hand." - Isaiah 41:10 CSB

"Though the mountains move and the hills shake, *my love will not be removed from you* and my covenant of peace will not be shaken," says your compassionate LORD." - Isaiah 54:10 CSB

"For I am persuaded that neither death nor life, nor angels nor rulers, nor things present nor things to come, nor powers, nor height nor depth, nor any other created thing will be able to separate us from the love of God that is in Christ Jesus our Lord." - Romans 8:38-39 CSB

• *Jesus and the Holy Spirit are with us always.*

"Jesus came near and said to them, "All authority has been given to me in heaven and on earth. Go, therefore, and make disciples of all nations, baptizing them in the name of the Father and of the Son and of the Holy Spirit, teaching them to observe everything I have commanded you. *And remember, I am with you always, to the end of the age.*" - Matthew 28:18-20 CSB

Summary:

1. You were created by God with a purpose. You were chosen before you were born. You are a unique creation made in the image of God and God knew you from the moment of your conception. Your parents may have been unaware of your conception but not God. Never doubt your significance.

2. God loves you. No matter how others may treat you, God always loves you.

3. Nothing can separate us from God.

4. God has a plan for your life – run your course not someone else's.

5. Always remember what waits at the finish line of the racecourse – eternity with Jesus. Your race may be difficult, but eternity will be worth it all.

6. To be happy you must hunger and thirst after righteousness.

Questions:

1. Why is it important to "love yourself" as Paul states in Romans 13? "The commandments, Do not commit adultery; do not murder; do not steal; do not covet; and any other commandment, are summed up by this commandment: *Love your neighbor as yourself.* Love does no wrong to a neighbor. Love, therefore, is the fulfillment of the law." - Romans 13:9-10 CSB.

2. What does Romans 8:38-39 mean to you when you are feeling down? "For I am persuaded that neither death nor life, nor angels nor rulers, nor things present nor things to come, nor powers, nor height nor depth, nor any other created thing will be able to separate us from the love of God that is in Christ Jesus our Lord." - Romans 8:38-39 CSB

3. What does it mean to be "treasured by God" as in Daniel 9?

4. How do you handle times of loneliness?

5. How do you understand what Jesus said to Peter in John 21:21-22? "When Peter saw him, he said to Jesus, "Lord, what about him? If I want him to remain until I come, Jesus answered, what is that to you? As for you, follow me."

6. Explain the importance of the order of this Beatitude. Is this the way the non-Christian attempts to be happy? "Blessed are those who hunger and thirst for righteousness, for they will be filled." - Matthew 5:6 CSB

7. How do you respond when people are bullying you?

Questions with suggested answers:

1. Why is it important to "love yourself" as Paul states in Romans 13? "The commandments, Do not commit adultery; do not murder; do not steal; do not covet; and any other commandment, are summed up by this commandment: *Love your neighbor as yourself*. Love does no wrong to a neighbor. Love, therefore, is the fulfillment of the law." - Romans 13:9-10 CSB.

Answer: Loving yourself is not a selfish concept, but rather a truth important to your self-esteem. Remember that God views us as individuals and wants to bless and build us up. Living in a world with billions of people may make us feel small and insignificant at times. God is so great that He can be God of all of us and yet personal. The little phrase "love your neighbor as yourself" is an interesting nugget of truth buried in Romans 13:9 that I had not seen before. That is, you are to "love yourself". We need enough self-love or self-esteem to see ourselves as we should—as a chosen child of the Almighty God—to then have the ability to respect and honor our neighbor.

2. What does Romans 8:38-39 mean to you when you are feeling down? "For I am persuaded that neither death nor life, nor angels nor rulers, nor things present nor things to come, nor powers, nor height nor depth, nor any other created thing will be able to separate us from the love of God that is in Christ Jesus our Lord." - Romans 8:38-39 CSB

Answer: There will be many times in our lives when things will not go our way. Perhaps we were born with a body shape and size that we are not happy about. Or maybe we want to have skills like someone else. The verses above reassure us that each of us was created by God as a unique person with a special mission on this earth. God loves us and we will never be separated from Him.

3. What does it mean to be "treasured by God" as in Daniel 9?

Answer: This verse and the other ones above make the case that although God is so big and powerful. He also is so all-caring that He cares and loves and treasures each of us every day. You can tell Him anything.

4. How do you handle times of loneliness?

Answer: Despite all the friends we may have on the internet, we still may be lonely. In addition to the verses above that reassure us that God is always with us, we need to see people in person not just on the phone. This means going to worship services on the weekend, join a small group, reach out to a lonely person and both of you will be uplifted. See *Mostly Scripture QD* days 282-284 for more verses.

5. How do you understand what Jesus said to Peter in John 21:21-22? "When Peter saw him, he said to Jesus, Lord, what about him? If I want him to remain until I come," Jesus answered, what is that to you? As for you, follow me."

Answer: This verse contains a very important truth that is easy to miss. Throughout school and the competitive workplace and world we live in we will compare ourselves to others. What is our class rank? What is the percentile rank on my score to get into grad school? How many papers did I publish? What was my batting average? How many sales did I produce compared to my colleagues? The list goes on and on. Jesus warns Peter here to not compare himself to John. Be satisfied with the way God made you; the talents and gifts He gave you; the body you were given and not always look at others and compare. Run your race and stay in your lane. Remember this verse, "Therefore, since we are surrounded by such a great cloud of witnesses, let us throw off everything that hinders and the sin that so easily entangles. *And let us run with perseverance the race marked out for us*," - Hebrews 12:1 NIV We are responsible to run the race, our race for the duration of our life on this earth and will then spend eternity with Jesus. It's a race individualized for you by God.

6. Explain the importance of the order of this Beatitude. Is this the way the nonChristian attempts to be happy? "Blessed are those who hunger and thirst for righteousness, for they will be filled." - Matthew 5:6 CSB

Answer: This is a tricky but very important verse. If you get this right, you will be happy says Jesus. This teaching is part of the Beatitudes that Jesus taught His disciples in the Sermon on the Mount. The teaching is complicated and for Christians. The word "blessed" means happy. All of us seek to be happy. The non-Christian focuses on things to make them happy – money, drugs, alcohol, dangerous stunts, opulent spending, gambling etc. But in the end, they are not happy. Jesus says to be happy you must "hunger and thirst for righteousness" then you will be happy and satisfied. Start to conduct yourself this way and see what happens to your level of happiness.

7. How do you respond when people are bullying you?

Answer: Bullying is when people make fun of the way God made you or your mission. Bullying is discussed in the Bible. There is the case of Hannah who was taunted by another woman for her inability to have a baby. As you read the story below notice the depression she experienced and how she responded with prayer. God answered her prayer with the birth of Samuel.

"Her rival would taunt her severely just to provoke her, because the LORD had kept Hannah from conceiving. Year after year, when she went up to the LORD's house, her rival taunted her in this way. Hannah would weep and would not eat. Hannah, why are you crying? Her husband Elkanah would ask. Why won't you eat? Why are you troubled? Am I not better to you than ten sons? On one occasion, Hannah got up after they ate and drank at Shiloh. The priest Eli was sitting on a chair by the doorpost of the LORD's temple. Deeply hurt, Hannah prayed to the LORD and wept with many tears. Making a vow, she pleaded, LORD of Armies, if you will take notice of your servant's affliction, remember and not forget me, and give your servant a son, I will give him to the LORD all the days of his life, and his hair will never be cut." - 1 Samuel 1:6-11 CSB

When I was growing up kids would occasionally taunt me. I was overweight and they called me "fatso". When I was in high school older guys would make fun of my immature physique in the locker room. For the most part I could laugh these off because I, with the help of my family and friends and church, had developed a solid sense of self-esteem based on God's love for me. Today, as a father, an uncle and grandfather I do not take bullying lightly. It's a big problem and the taunts are much more severe than 'fatso'. The defensive strategies today as outlined in the Bible remain similar – if you know who you are in God's eyes you can withstand quite a bit of abusive language. But it is still really uncomfortable and depressing. If you are experiencing that at your school or work, I would encourage you to share the experience with friends and family and like Hannah pray to the LORD of Armies. Read the verses and have a clear understanding of how important you are in God's eyes and that He designed you with a purpose. Sometimes it helps to try to get "inside the head" of the person taunting you. What is driving them to taunt you? Often it is because they are insecure and need to make themselves feel better by putting others down below them. Once you understand their weakness, you actually may have pity on them. Lastly, teachers and parents must tackle this problem head-on. It's not trivial.

2

How to Know the Will of God

There are many key decisions to be made in life. Should I go to college? Where? What major? Should I get married? To whom? When? What job? Where should we live? Should we have children? When is the best time? In most everyday situations, it is not necessary to pray about what to do. After all God has given us a brain and He expects us to use it. However, the more important decisions need to be discussed with the eternal God who has a plan for each of our lives. The Bible has much advice on this subject and provides excellent examples for the Christ-follower to model. These principles are organized into 18 steps.

Step 1. Put first things first — dedicate yourself to God; become a Christ-follower and listen to God's Word. To know the will of God you need to know who God is, His nature, and His characteristics. Trusting God and His attributes will shape your prayers. In brief, the "first things first" approach involves:

• *Believe in Jesus — to do the will of God requires knowing Him.*
"What can we do to perform the works of God? " they asked. Jesus replied, "*This is the work of God -- that you believe in the one he has sent*." - John 6:28-29 CSB

• *Be dedicated to God; be serious about your faith like the Macedonians. To discern God's direction, they dedicated themselves to the Lord.*
"Best of all, they went beyond our highest hopes, for their first action was to dedicate themselves to the Lord and to us for whatever directions God might give them." 2 Corinthians 8:5, NLT.

• *Make God's will your goal; focus on His will not yours.*
"Therefore, since Christ suffered in the flesh, arm yourselves also with the same understanding -- because the one who suffers in the flesh is finished with sin -- in order

to live the remaining time in the flesh no longer for human desires, but for God's will."
- 1 Peter 4:1-2 CSB

• *Be purpose driven. Notice Paul's burning desire for doing God's will.*
"But I consider my life of no value to myself; *my purpose is to finish my course* and the
ministry I received from the Lord Jesus, to testify to the gospel of God's grace." - Acts
20:24 CSB

**• *If you delight yourself in the things of God then your desires will match up with God's
will.*** If you are a Christian, then you will naturally have a desire to know and do the will
of God. You will want to seek that will in every area of your life whether it be your
vocation, your choice of spouse and where you will live.

"Take delight in the LORD, and he will give you your heart's desires. Commit your way
to the LORD; trust in him, and he will act, making your righteousness shine like the
dawn, your justice like the noonday." - Psalm 37:4-6 CSB

**• *Listen and follow the commands of the LORD as written in the Bible. This is the great
"Eagle's wings speech" God gave to Moses.***
"Moses went up the mountain to God, and the LORD called to him from the mountain:
This is what you must say to the house of Jacob and explain to the Israelites: You have
seen what I did to the Egyptians and *how I carried you on eagles' wings* and brought you
to myself. *Now if you will carefully listen to me and keep my covenant, you will be my own
possession out of all the peoples, although the whole earth is mine, and you will be my
kingdom of priests and my holy nation.* These are the words that you are to say to the
Israelites." - Exodus 19:3-6 CSB

Questions:

1. How do you understand and apply Psalm 37:4 to "take delight in the LORD"? Do
you believe that God indeed wants you to have "your heart's desire"?

2. What are the key areas of your life right now that you would like to know the will of
God? Is it college? Career? Marriage? Have children? Job switch? Get the next COVID-
19 vaccine?

3. Is the topic of your question for God's direction already clearly described in the Bible?

4. What about areas that are not clear in the Bible? How do I obey my conscience? Could my conscience be different than others and still be consistent with the Bible?

5. Jack and Jill fall in love and decide they want to move in with each other before they get married to save rent money. It's a one-bedroom apartment and they plan to share the bed. This situation is called 'co-habitation' or 'living together'. As their friend, they ask if you think that's ok? They come to your church and profess to be believers. Is this something that could be "the will of God?" Is it worth praying about?

6. You are visiting a high school friend who is now at a college in another city. At dinner she serves all vegetarian dishes."I no longer eat meat because I now feel it is not fair to the animals." What would you do?

7. What other thorny conscience issues can you think of where Christians might disagree? Dress…movies…books to read. Discuss these.

8. It is important to interpret Acts 20:24 correctly. Read it again and discuss it. What is Paul saying here and what is he NOT saying? "But I consider my life of no value to myself; my purpose is to finish my course and the ministry I received from the Lord Jesus, to testify to the gospel of God's grace." - Acts 20:24 CSB

Questions with suggested answers:

1. How do you understand and apply Psalm 37:4 to "take delight in the LORD"? Do you believe that God indeed wants you to have "your heart's desire"?

Answer: This is a very important verse, but it may be difficult to understand if you do not think it through. If you are truly 'delighting in the LORD' you will be in such close fellowship with God that your heart's desires will be in synchrony with God's will. It is important to realize that the eternal, 'all-knowing, all-powerful" God wants your best. Let me give you two examples. When I was in college my best friend (and brother in Christ) expressed concern to me that "God is going to make me marry someone who I don't want to marry"! Little did I know at the time that he was in love with my sister, but he was afraid that God would not make it happen. Both he and my sister walked closely with the LORD and indeed God gave them the desires of their hearts and they have been happily married over 45 years. A second example comes from my 92-year-old mother, now widowed, living in assisted living. My brother and I carefully manage her money because of her concern about it running out before she dies. I often tell her "Mom, you have plenty of money – you can do anything you want!" She usually replies, "How can you say that?" "Because I know what you delight in, and you will not be spending it on anything extravagant!" Her desires at this point in life are entirely in synch with God's. She goes to church, prays, and reads her Bible every day, watches sports and news on TV, and takes us out to eat at when we visit. Her primary delights are her family and her relationship with Jesus. No cruises, no fancy cars etc. So, to effectively do the will of God you need to focus on 'knowing God' *so that your natural delights will be consistent with His will.*

2. What are the key areas of your life right now that you would like to know the will of God? Is it college? Career? Marriage? Have children? Job switch? Get the COVID-19 vaccine?

Answer: As you look to God for answers also remember to know your own gifts and physical abilities that God has given you. What do you like to do? Your God-given talents and desires are a real clue as to what God wants for you. I like this quote from Rick Warren in his classic book *The Purpose Driven Life* "You will be most effective when you use your spiritual gifts and abilities in the area of your heart's desire and in a way that best expresses your personality and experiences. The better the fit, the more successful you will be."

3. Is the topic of your question for God's direction already clearly described in the Bible?

Answer: Many times, our questions about "the will of God" has already been answered in the Bible. If it is, then you do not need to ask for God's will – He already told you! So, before searching too far look in the Bible. A good example is the Ten Commandments in Exodus 20. *The 10 Commandments are a clear example of many issues that you do not need to pray about but rather obey implicitly.*

Peter also gives a list of key areas that he says are to be avoided.

"For there has already been enough time spent in doing what the Gentiles choose to do: carrying on in *unrestrained behavior, evil desires, drunkenness, orgies, carousing, and lawless idolatry.*" - 1 Peter 4:3 CSB

4. What about areas that are not clear in the Bible? How do I obey my conscience? Could my conscience be different than others and still be consistent with the Bible?

Answer: A good example is "what can I eat"? The Bible actually talks a lot about diet. The original diet as described in Genesis was all fruits, vegetables, and grain. Then after sin entered the world meat was allowed. The Bible says we can decide what we want to eat – and we should obey our conscience in this matter.
Romans 14:1-3, Hebrews 13:18

"I always strive to have a clear conscience toward God and men." - Acts 24:16 CSB

5. Jack and Jill fall in love and decide they want to move in with each other before they get married to save rent money. It's a one-bedroom apartment and they plan to share the bed. This situation is called 'co-habitation' or 'living together'. As their friend, they ask if you think that's ok? They come to your church and profess to be believers. Is this something that could be "the will of God?" Is it worth praying about?

Answer: Jack sleeping in the same bed with Jill before marriage falls into the category of being contrary to the written will of God because it will be a great temptation to commit sexual sin before Biblical marriage. Other examples are getting drunk, stealing something, or lying. These are obvious violations of God's will and there is no need to "pray about whether to do it or not". These are difficult temptations because all of them can feel very pleasurable physically in the moment but later when guilt sets in, they are very distressing and produce regret and anxiety.

6. You are visiting a high school friend who is now at a college in another city. At dinner she serves all vegetarian dishes. "I no longer eat meat because I now feel it is not fair to the animals." What would you do?

Answer: This is a "right of conscience" issue and the Bible accepts both ways. See Romans 14 above. No need to argue or pray about it – God's will has already been written and accepts both ways.

7. What other thorny conscience issues can you think of where Christians might disagree? Dress…movies…books to read…what version of the Bible to read. Discuss these.

Answer: Discuss in the group.

8. It is important to interpret Acts 20:24 correctly. Read it again and discuss it. What is Paul saying here and what is he NOT saying? "But I consider my life of no value to

myself; my purpose is to finish my course and the ministry I received from the Lord Jesus, to testify to the gospel of God's grace." - Acts 20:24 CSB

Answer: This verse is about having a purpose-driven life. Paul was really focused on listening to the Holy Spirit and doing God's will. He often did not have clarity on what was coming next, and neither will we. What this verse is not saying is that he did not care about his life – he wasn't stupid, and he was not reckless. Never use this verse to support reckless actions. But what we should do is focus on the purpose for us marked out by God. That means we invest our money in the things of God rather than the things that are only pleasurable to others.

Step 2: Stay focused; learn from the past but mainly move forward.

"Let your eyes look forward; fix your gaze straight ahead. Carefully consider the path for your feet, and all your ways will be established. Don't turn to the right or to the left; keep your feet away from evil." - Proverbs 4:25-27 CSB

• *Move forward and stay on-task. Moses said this to the Israelites after reminding them of the 10 Commandments in Deuteronomy 5.*
"Be careful to do as the LORD your God has commanded you; you are not to turn aside to the right or the left. Follow the whole instruction the LORD your God has commanded you, so that you may live, prosper, and have a long life in the land you will possess." - Deuteronomy 5:32-33 CSB

Step 3: Remember that God is "for us" – He wants the best for us. He will not abandon you, but the will of God may seem at times to be hard to understand.

"*A person's steps are established by the LORD, and he takes pleasure in his way*. Though he falls, he will not be overwhelmed, because the LORD supports him with his hand. I have been young and now I am old, yet I have not seen the righteous abandoned or his children begging for bread. He is always generous, always lending, and his children are a blessing. - Psalm 37:23-26, Psalm 57:2, Psalm 16:11

"You have revealed the paths of life to me; you will fill me with gladness in your presence." - Acts 2:28 CSB

Step 4. Renew your mind so that you will be able to clearly discern the will of God in the matter. Never make an important decision when you are not in communication with God or if you are currently living your life outside His will.

"Do not be conformed to this age, but *be transformed by the renewing of your mind, so that you may discern what is the good, pleasing, and perfect will of God.*" - Romans 12:2 CSB

Step 5. Ask for help and advice from others you trust. Avoid the mistake of going ahead with a decision without asking God. Do not be stubborn.

• Joshua and the Israelites prepared for battle with the Gibeonites by stocking up with food and weapons, but they did not seek out the Lord's will and were deceived.
"Then the men of Israel *took some of their provisions* but *did not seek the LORD's decision.*" - Joshua 9:14 CSB

• Solomon advised to listen to counsel.
"Listen to counsel and receive instruction so that you may be wise later in life." - Proverbs 19:20 CSB

• Be like King Uzziah who learned from Zechariah to trust God and always seek guidance from Him.
"Uzziah sought God during the days of Zechariah, *who taught him to fear God. And as long as the king sought guidance from the LORD, God gave him success.*" - 2 Chronicles 26:5 NLT

• God can use even animals to reveal His will. This story of Balaam and the donkey illustrates how stubbornness interferes with learning the will of God. Also, it teaches that we do not always know what is going on behind the scenes of a situation.
Numbers 22:22-34 CSB

• David also warns of being stubborn about the will of God.
"The LORD says, "I will guide you along the best pathway for your life. I will advise you and watch over you. Do not be like a senseless horse or mule that needs a bit and bridle to keep it under control." Many sorrows come to the wicked, but unfailing love surrounds those who trust the LORD." Psalm 32:8-10, NLT."

• *Understand your need for God's wisdom on your prayer request.*
"Now if any of you lacks wisdom, he should ask God -- who gives to all generously and ungrudgingly -- and it will be given to him." - James 1:5 CSB

Step 6. Be patient and be willing to wait if the answer is not coming. God does not always act fast, and waiting is common and part of the normal process. If we run ahead of God, we are likely to make the wrong decision.

• *The Israelites were often guilty of impatience as described below by David. Do not test God or frustrate Him – you may get something you do not want.*
"They soon forgot his works and would not wait for his counsel. They were seized with craving in the wilderness and tested God in the desert. *He gave them what they asked for but sent a wasting disease among them.*" - Psalm 106:13-15 CSB

• *Waiting is not always wasted time. God's timing is always the best time. This waiting may be long and require endurance. Try to look at the situation with the "long view". Maintain hope throughout the process.*
"He has made *everything appropriate in its time.* He has also put eternity in their hearts, but no one can discover the work God has done from beginning to end." - Ecclesiastes 3:11 CSB
Isaiah 30:18

"Now in this hope we were saved, but hope that is seen is not hope, because who hopes for what he sees? Now if we hope for what we do not see, *we eagerly wait for it with patience.*" - Romans 8:24-25 CSB

Romans 15:4 CSB

• *If it's a financial opportunity or question you are praying about remember Solomon's advice.*
"Develop your business first before building your house." Proverbs 24:27, NLT.

Question with suggested answer:

1. Why is it sometimes difficult to wait for an answer from God? How do you know when it is time to proceed with a decision?

Answer: Waiting is tough sometimes (actually always). The following is great advice from Jan Johnson, author, and speaker (https://janjohnson.org/), "Waiting on God is a problem only if you're in a relationship with God for utilitarian purposes –to get the prize from the vending machine. *But if you're in the relationship for God Himself, waiting means you still have what you want – God – even while you wait.*" Jan Johnson, "When the Soul Listens".

Step 7. The will of God is personal and is an individualized plan for you.

• *David speaks about "your path".*
"Trust in the LORD with all your heart, and do not rely on your own understanding; in all your ways know him, and he will make your paths straight." - Proverbs 3:5-6 CSB

• *Jesus explained this principle for Peter when he was concerned about what was going to happen to his colleague John.*
"Peter turned around and saw behind them the disciple Jesus loved--the one who had leaned over to Jesus during supper and asked, "Lord, who will betray you?" Peter asked Jesus, "What about him, Lord?" Jesus replied, "If I want him to remain alive until I return, what is that to you? *As for you, follow me.*" - John 21:20-22 NLT

• *God's plans for Paul were very specific – "you are going to the Gentiles", "You are going to Rome".*
"He said to me, 'Go, because I will send you far away to the Gentiles.' " - Acts 22:21 CSB

Acts 23:11 CSB

• *Moses dearly wanted to go into the Promised Land, but God said "No, Joshua will be the one to take them, not you."*
"At that time I begged the LORD: Lord GOD, you have begun to show your greatness and your strong hand to your servant, for what god is there in heaven or on earth who can perform deeds and mighty acts like yours? Please let me cross over and see the beautiful land on the other side of the Jordan, that good hill country and Lebanon. But the LORD was angry with me because of you and would not listen to me. The LORD said to me, 'That's enough! Do not speak to me again about this matter. Go to the top of Pisgah and look to the west, north, south, and east, and see it with your own eyes, for you will not cross the Jordan. But commission Joshua and encourage and strengthen him, for he will cross over ahead of the people and enable them to inherit this land that you will see." - Deuteronomy 3:23-28 CSB

Step 8. Consider whether the request is consistent with your spiritual gifts? We were made to contribute not consume.

Romans 12:1-8 CSB

Step 9. Actively ask; explore the options; count the cost; expect an answer. Determining God's will is a dynamic process.

• *We are seeking God's will, not our will or the will of others. Jesus sought His Father's will – we should too.*
"I can do nothing on my own. I judge only as I hear, and my judgment is just, because *I do not seek my own will, but the will of him who sent me."* - John 5:30 CSB
Philippians 2:12-13

• *Have faith that God can indeed answer your prayer; don't doubt. Seek to understand His will even if you do not immediately agree with it.*
"Now if any of you lacks wisdom, *he should ask God* -- who gives to all generously and ungrudgingly -- and it will be given to him. *But let him ask in faith without doubting.* For the doubter is like the surging sea, driven and tossed by the wind. That person should not expect to receive anything from the Lord, being double-minded and unstable in all his ways." - James 1:5-8 CSB
Ephesians 5:17

• *Ask, seek, and knock. These are action words.*
"*Ask*, and it will be given to you. *Seek*, and you will find. *Knock*, and the door will be opened to you. For everyone who asks receives, and the one who seeks finds, and to the one who knocks, the door will be opened." - Matthew 7:7-8 CSB

"Trust in the LORD with all your heart; do not depend on your own understanding. *Seek* his will in all you do, and he will direct your paths." Proverbs 3:5, 6, NLT.
James 4:2

• *Ask with the correct motives.*
"You ask and don't receive because you ask with wrong motives, so that you may spend it on your pleasures." - James 4:3 CSB

• *Explore the options, investigate, learn. The Israelites did this before entering the Promised Land.*

"Then all of you approached me and said, 'Let's send men ahead of us, so that they may explore the land for us and bring us back a report about the route we should go up and the cities we will come to.' "The plan seemed good to me, so I selected twelve men from among you, one man for each tribe. They left and went up into the hill country and came to the Valley of Eshcol, scouting the land. They took some of the fruit from the land in their hands, carried it down to us, and brought us back a report: The land the LORD our God is giving us is good." - Deuteronomy 1:22-25 CSB

Step 10. Go where God is working. Where is He leading? Where is He calling you to? What's hot (open)? What's not (closed)?

"If anyone serves me, *he must follow me*. Where I am, there my servant also will be. If anyone serves me, the Father will honor him." - John 12:26 CSB

• *Follow Me – there are many verses where Jesus told the person to follow Him. What does that mean? It means you must pay attention to where Jesus is going. Following requires going places and taking jobs where Jesus is moving and working.*
"*Follow me*," Jesus told them, "and I will make you fish for people." - Mark 1:17 CSB

"Then Jesus said to his disciples, "If anyone wants to follow after me, let him deny himself, take up his cross, and follow me." - Matthew 16:24 CSB

• *Be sensitive to the calling of the Holy Spirit. The case of Barnabas and Saul, missionaries sent out by the Holy Spirit via the local Church.*
Acts 13:1-5

• *Sometimes the Holy Spirit will compel you without a clear vision of the future. That is the risk associated with following Jesus. The verse below is in reference to the Apostle Paul.*
"And now I am on my way to Jerusalem, compelled by the Spirit, not knowing what I will encounter there," - Acts 20:22 CSB

• *When God closes a door, He often opens a new one. This is what Moses told the Israelites after they left Egypt.*
"And he brought us out from there, that he might bring us in and give us the land that he swore to give to our fathers." - Deuteronomy 6:23 ESV

Questions:

1. We all have to avoid the trap of comparing ourselves to others. How does this verse help you avoid that? "Peter asked Jesus, "What about him, Lord?" Jesus replied, "If I want him to remain alive until I return, what is that to you? You follow me"." John 21:21, 22, NLT."

2. What are some situations where you have struggled with comparisons?

3. What does it mean when someone says, "I am called to…"?

4. What did Jesus mean in Matthew 16:24, when He said "…let him deny himself"?

5. What role does your own planning and research have in determining the will of God?

Questions with suggested answers:

1. We all have to avoid the trap of comparing ourselves to others. How does this verse help you avoid that? "Peter asked Jesus, "What about him, Lord?" Jesus replied, "If I want him to remain alive until I return, what is that to you? You follow me"." John 21:21, 22, NLT."

Answer: Peter and John were good friends and colleagues. They had been through a lot with each other. Yet, Jesus said Peter was not to be concerned with the plan for John but rather to focus on the plan for Peter. Indeed, Peter dies a martyr and John lives a long life and writes the book of Revelation on the Isle of Patmos.

2. What are some situations where you have struggled with comparisons?

Answer: We often compare ourselves to others even within our own family. Of course, it can be useful to learn from others and emulate them or their style but in the end as we have discussed above, you are a unique creation of God with unique talents and a unique purpose. I sometimes use a honeybee analogy when speaking to my young interns and residents, "you are going to work with a lot of professors as you go through your training. Be like a honeybee that samples and collects nectar from many flowers but makes its own honey. Take the best from all of us but be your style."

3. What does it mean when someone says, "I am called to…"?

Answer: In the example provided in Acts 13 we that the Holy Spirit working through the local Church called Barnabas and Saul (aka Paul) to be missionaries and preach about Jesus in foreign lands. The Church is *to call and send* and as part of that process it, the Church, fasts and prays and supports the "sent out" ones. Does the church you go to send out missionaries? This is a sign of a church that cares about telling others about Jesus.

Now, each of us has a "calling". Your specific calling may be to stay home and serve the Lord locally by providing support for the missionaries. You should feel called to the occupation that you are in, and it should be consistent with your spiritual gifts. Eric Liddell was a devoted Christian and a runner in the 1924 Paris Olympic games and a devoted Christian. Watch the movie *Chariots of Fire* sometime. His famous quote, "I believe God made me for a purpose, but he also made me fast! And when I run I feel his pleasure." After the Olympics he became a missionary to China and died there of an inoperable brain tumor in 1945.

There are a number of verses on "calling" – look them up in your Bible. For example, Paul says "live up to what God has called you to do"."Therefore I, the prisoner in the Lord, *urge you to live worthy of the calling you have received*," - Ephesians 4:1 CSB

4. What did Jesus mean in Matthew 16:24, when He said "…let him deny himself"?

Answer: If you are a "Christ-follower" and you are indeed committed to "following Jesus" in the way He leads you, then you will sometimes need to "deny" what you want to do in favor of what God wants you to do. Can you think of instances where that has happened in your life?

5. What role does your own planning and research have in determining the will of God?

Answer: The example from Numbers 13 (and Deuteronomy 1 mentioned above) is a great example of researching the subject that you need to decide on.

"When Moses sent them to scout out the land of Canaan, he told them, "Go up this way to the Negev, then go up into the hill country."See what the land is like, and whether the people who live there are strong or weak, few or many."Is the land they live in good or bad? Are the cities they live in encampments or fortifications? "Is the land fertile or unproductive? Are there trees in it or not? Be courageous. Bring back some fruit from the land." It was the season for the first ripe grapes." - Numbers 13:17-20 CSB

Can you think of some examples from your life? One easy one is deciding which house to buy or apartment to rent. Although we pray about it, we also count the cost, is it the right fit, is the location safe and close to my work etc. We scout it all out. Before deciding to launch into a new research project we do the preparation work. Jesus also mentioned the importance of "counting the cost" in Luke 14 "For which of you, wanting to build a tower, doesn't first sit down and calculate the cost to see if he has enough to complete it? "Otherwise, after he has laid the foundation and cannot finish it, all the onlookers will begin to ridicule him, "saying, 'This man started to build and wasn't able to finish.' " - Luke 14:28-30 CSB

Step 11. Focus on the next step in the decision process - not the whole journey. When we seek the will of God in a matter, we often want the "whole plan" when God is likely to reveal only the next move to make. I liken this concept to what happens when you are driving or biking and suddenly you hit a patch of fog and the road or trail becomes so hard to see. You must slow down and focus only on the portion of the road illuminated by your headlights. Once you get around the bend the next section of the road becomes illuminated. It is often that way with discerning the next step in God's will. He is unlikely to reveal the entire plan for you in one chunk. In fact, if He did it may be very frightening! He knows what you need and can handle at the place in life you are at.

I often use the quote from Hubert Humphrey, former Vice President of the United States, and a US Senator from the state of Minnesota - "Never make an important decision until you have to." It's a great way to deal with difficult decisions – wait until the way is clear (or at least a bit clearer) and the decision will be easier.

• *A good example from the Bible is Saul (Paul) after his conversion on the road to Damascus. God revealed only the next step, which was very clear in its instruction, but He did not tell Saul the whole plan.*
"I said, What shall I do, Lord? And the Lord told me, Get up and go into Damascus, and there you will be told all that you are to do." Acts 22:10, NLT.
Acts 22:21

• *Understand the importance of the LORD being in your plans. He is your ultimate Counselor. Are you consulting with Him every day?*
"Unless the LORD builds a house, its builders labor over it in vain; unless the LORD watches over a city, the watchman stays alert in vain." - Psalm 127:1 CSB

• *God is interested in us knowing His will – this is the advantage of being a follower of Jesus.*
"The secret counsel of the LORD is for those who fear him, and he reveals his covenant to them." - Psalm 25:14 CSB

Step 12. Look for the open door and don't fret over closed doors. Closed doors may be hard to accept but they represent clear answers to your search for the will of God.

• *Thank God for open doors.*
"When I came to the city of Troas to preach the Good News of Christ, *the Lord opened a door of opportunity for me.*" - 2 Corinthians 2:12 NLT
Colossians 4:3, Acts 14:27

• *An open door for you may be opposed by others. Opposition by others is not always a reliable test of God's will. This can be tricky because we want the advice of others yet here it states that even if the door is open, you still may encounter resistance.*
"Because a wide door for effective ministry has opened for me -- *yet many oppose me.*" - 1 Corinthians 16:9 CSB

• *Open doors may eventually close; don't persist too long – move on to more productive fields. Paul in Athens.*
"Paul entered the synagogue and spoke boldly over a period of three months, arguing and persuading them about the kingdom of God. *But when some became hardened and would not believe, slandering the Way in front of the crowd, he withdrew from them,* taking the disciples, and conducted discussions every day in the lecture hall of Tyrannus. This went on for two years, so that all the residents of Asia, both Jews and Greeks, heard the word of the Lord." - Acts 19:8-10 CSB

• *Accept closed doors even though you may never know why. The Case of Paul and closed doors in Asia and Mysia. Note here that no reason was given – they tried, things seemed right, but the Holy Spirit prevented them. This is a classic case of seeking the will of God by testing the door, finding it closed, and moving on.*

"They went through the region of Phrygia and Galatia; they had been forbidden by the Holy Spirit to speak the word in Asia. When they came to Mysia, they tried to go into Bithynia, *but the Spirit of Jesus did not allow them.*" - Acts 16:6-7 CSB

Dr. Martyn-Lloyd Jones says regarding this verse that the will of the Holy Spirit is the ultimate arbitrator on determining the will of God. We may think all things are right with a decision we are making but if "it does seem right, but you feel the Spirit is against it, hesitate with moving on." (paraphrased from his sermon on Romans 1:7-15 February 3, 1956, available on MLJ Trust).

Question with suggested answer:

1. While waiting to understand the direction God wants you to take, you will usually have to make some sort of "move". That might be applying for a position, trying out a job as a temporary employee, doing some research. If you then get accepted or you like it this may be interpreted as an "open door". On the other hand, if you get turned down this is called a "closed door". Describe a time when you used this strategy. Did it work?

Answer: Many situations require an application, and the decision may be made for you. We call this the concept of the open vs closed door. For example, a job promotion opportunity is posted, and you decide to apply. You prayerfully fill out the application and pray that God will allow you to get the job. The decision that comes back after all applicants have been interviewed may or may not be what you desired but it does clarify God's will. Most of the time a closed door, although disheartening, is a clear answer. An open door usually means that God wants you to move through it and take the next step.

Step 13. Timing is critical - Focus on the times you are living in - your generation.

• *We serve God in a specific time and era – that is our responsibility. Don't wish that you lived in the past or even the future – focus on the current situation.*
"Now this is not a reference to David, for *after David had served his generation according to the will of God*, he died and was buried, and his body decayed." Acts 13:36, NLT.

For us, at the time of this writing in 2023, it is the great COVID-19 pandemic of 2020-2023+. In 2022 - 23 it was the Russian invasion of Ukraine, monkeypox, the return of inflation, plummeting stock market, high gas prices, devastating earthquakes in Turkey and Morocco. We had no choice in these events. For many it was death and disease or loss of a job or displacement.

Step 14. Follow God rather than go out ahead of Him. Pay attention to the obvious; discerning God's will can sometimes be easy. Don't make it hard. God sometimes makes it very clear what He wants us to do.

• *God leads us. Notice how David prays this in the 23rd Psalm.*
[[A Psalm of David.]] The LORD [is] my shepherd; I shall not want. He maketh me to lie down in green pastures: *he leadeth me* beside the still waters. He restoreth my soul: *he leadeth me* in the paths of righteousness for his name's sake. - Psalm 23:1-3 KJV

• *Noah is an example of "walking with God". He followed; never walked ahead.*
"These are the family records of Noah. Noah was a righteous man, blameless among his contemporaries; *Noah walked with God.*" - Genesis 6:9 CSB

• *Follow the "cloud" – it was an obvious sign from God as to whether to "go or stay put".*
"Then the cloud covered the Tabernacle, and the glorious presence of the LORD filled it. Moses was no longer able to enter the Tabernacle because the cloud had settled down over it, and the Tabernacle was filled with the awesome glory of the LORD. *Now whenever the cloud lifted from the Tabernacle and moved, the people of Israel would set out on their journey, following it.* But if the cloud stayed, they would stay until it moved again." Exodus 40:34-37, NLT.

• *Moses told the Israelites that God goes before them.*
"The *LORD your God who goes before you will fight for you*, just as you saw him do for you in Egypt." - Deuteronomy 1:30 CSB

• *The voice of God can be very clear; never drown it out.*
Genesis 26:1-5

• The will of God can be life-changing, like it was for Abram and Moses. God gave them orders and they followed.

"The LORD said to Abram: Go out from your land, your relatives, and your father's house to the land that I will show you." - Genesis 12:1 CSB

Question with suggested answer:

1. I sometimes get stuck in determining the will of God over a matter. What if I follow God faithfully but I cannot discern a clear answer to my question as to which way to go with a decision?

Answer: Walking with God implies "movement" and sometimes when it is not exactly clear what to do you have to decide to do something (get moving) and then it may become clearer if this is the correct one. I will give you several examples that have helped me. If you are in a stationary boat and want to go in a certain direction you cannot steer the boat until you start moving. Thus, if you are stuck with a decision just start moving on the decision and then you will be able to steer. Have you ever been hiking or biking and come to a fork or turn with several options and the map is unclear? You look at the blinking spot on your GPS phone and then at the trail – which way? I often just pick one of the options and start moving or riding and then after a minute or so look again at the GPS and see if I made the right choice. Moving provides clarity. Lastly, try the open vs closed door approach. Should I go to College X or College Y? What is God's will? Well, apply to both and see which of the two even accept you. Maybe one will reject your application (closed door) and the other will accept you (open door).

Step 15. Pray but don't demand to get what you want. Remember, what you ultimately want is "God's will" not "your will".

• The case of the three men in the fiery furnace.

"Shadrach, Meshach, and Abednego replied, "O Nebuchadnezzar, we do not need to defend ourselves before you. If we are thrown into the blazing furnace, the God whom we serve is able to save us. He will rescue us from your power, Your Majesty. *But even if he doesn't,* Your Majesty can be sure that we will never serve your gods or worship the gold statue you have set up"." Daniel 3:16-18, NLT.

• *Jesus prayed about doing the will of God; He focused intently on His mission.*
"But I do nothing without consulting the Father. I judge as I am told. And my judgment is absolutely just, because *it is according to the will of God who sent me*; it is not merely my own." John 5:30, NLT.
John 4:32, 34

• *Pray even when we are stressed out and cannot even clearly express our needs to God. The Holy Spirit will interpret our needs to God the Father. He will also align our requests with God's will.*
"And the Holy Spirit helps us in our weakness. For example, we don't know what God wants us to pray for. But the Holy Spirit prays for us with groanings that cannot be expressed in words. And the Father who knows all hearts knows what the Spirit is saying, for the Spirit pleads for us believers in harmony with God's own will. And we know that God causes everything to work together for the good of those who love God and are called according to his purpose for them." - Romans 8:26-28 NLT
1 Corinthians 2:10-12 NLT

• *Be persistent. This is a verse to be memorized.*
"One day Jesus told his disciples a story to show that *they should always pray and never give up*." - Luke 18:1 NLT

Step 16. Be ready for doubts and not always happy results. Sometimes there is trouble despite doing the will of God.

• *Example of Moses when trouble came despite doing what God wanted.*
"Then Moses went back to the LORD and protested, Why have you brought all this trouble on your own people, Lord? Why did you send me? Ever since I came to Pharaoh as your spokesman, he has been even more brutal to your people. And you have done nothing to rescue them!" - Exodus 5:22-23 NLT

• *Example of Paul*
"And now I stand on trial because of the hope in what God promised to our ancestors, "the promise our twelve tribes hope to reach as they earnestly serve him night and day. King Agrippa, I am being accused by the Jews because of this hope." - Acts 26:6-7 CSB

• *Example of Joseph - things looked bad for him when he was sold to the Egyptians, but it was all part of grand plan that he could not see at the beginning.*

"The patriarchs became jealous of Joseph and sold him into Egypt, but God was with him and rescued him out of all his troubles. He gave him favor and wisdom in the sight of Pharaoh, king of Egypt, who appointed him ruler over Egypt and over his whole household." - Acts 7:9-10 CSB

• *Sometimes the will of God is associated with a "but"—the case of Paul and the shipwreck. The will of God may not always initially be a good result from an earthly perspective for us.*

"So take courage! For I believe God. It will be just as he said. *But we will be shipwrecked on an island.*" Acts 27:25, 26, NLT."

Question with suggested answer:

1. Have you ever moved ahead with what was clearly the will of God and it did not work out? How did that feel?

Answer: This is a common problem. I recall a family from our church who felt the call to work with refugees in a foreign country. They were sent out by our church with full support and encouragement. They quit their jobs in the US, went to language school, and then moved. They were over in this foreign land for only a few months when the COVID-19 pandemic spread throughout the world and the specific nation they were serving in. The disease ruined the plans to work with refugees and they returned home. Why did this happen? Were they wrong to have gone there in the first place? Some answers will never be revealed to us this side of eternity.

Step 17. Remember that doing the will of God is associated with eternal life. God wants you to please Him and to focus on eternity. That is more important to God than your work being 'productive'.

"And this world is fading away, along with everything that people crave. *But anyone who does what pleases God will live forever.*" - 1 John 2:17 NLT

• *Evaluate the will of God in the totality of your life not just one isolated request.* If we are believers, then the promise is that God works synergistically in all the events of your life. He takes multiple events (both good and bad) and works them out for our good.

This verse does NOT say all things are good. Rather, it says God takes them all and works them for eternal good.

"We know that all things work together for the good of those who love God, who are called according to his purpose." - Romans 8:28 CSB

Question with suggested answer:

1. How can Romans 8:28 be misused? Can you give an example?

Answer: Sometimes people take a tragic event and apply this verse. It is important to remember that the event itself may not be good at all – it may be very tragic. For example, when my wife was 18 years old her mother was killed instantly in a car accident leaving her Dad an immediate widower with 8 children. This verse was mentioned. Her family did understand the meaning and never became bitter against God. But now some 50 years later we have no better understanding of why the tragic accident happened. Now God did work in the family and the community and church were a marvelous support. All children became Christ followers, but several suffered significant emotional damage from the loss of their mother at a young age. What was God doing here? Why? We have decided that the answer to that question will come only when we get to Heaven. It is important to always focus on our eternal hope.

Step 18. Stay with the plan—the case of Paul and the Corinthians.

"We will not boast about things done outside our area of authority. *We will boast only about what has happened within the boundaries of the work God has given us*, which includes our working with you." - 2 Corinthians 10:13 NLT

Summary of the 18 Steps to understanding God's will. It's an adventure that is lived out every day. Enjoy it – it's exciting.

Step 1. Put first things first – dedicate yourself to God; become a Christ-follower and listen to God's Word.

Step 2: Stay focused; learn from the past but move forward.

Step 3: Remember that God is "for us" – He wants the best for us. He will not abandon you, although the will of God may seem hard to understand at the time.

Step 4. Renew your mind so that you will be able to clearly discern the will of God in the matter. Never make an important decision when you are not in communication with God or if you are currently living your life outside His will.

Step 5. Ask for help and advice from others you trust. Avoid the mistake of going ahead with a decision without asking God. Do not be stubborn.

Step 6. Be patient and be willing to wait if the answer is not coming.

Step 7. The will of God is personal and is an individualized plan for you.

Step 8. Consider whether the request is consistent with your spiritual gifts? You were made to contribute not consume.

Step 9. Actively ask; explore the options; count the cost; expect an answer. Determining God's will is a dynamic process.

Step 10. Go where God is working. Where is that? What's hot?

Step 11. Focus on the next step in the decision process - not the whole journey.

Step 12. Look for the open door and don't fret over closed doors – they can be clear answers.

Step 13. Focus on the time you are living in – timing is critical.

Step 14. Follow God rather than go out ahead of Him. Pay attention to the obvious

Step 15. Pray but don't demand.

Step 16. Be ready for doubts and not always happy results.

Step 17. Remember that doing the will of God is associated with eternal life.

Step 18. Stay with the plan—the case of Paul and the Corinthians.

3

How to Deal with Temptation

A temptation is the desire to do something, to take a specific action. It is an enticement to sin. The tempting aspect comes from Satan and in itself is not sin; rather, the sin is yielding or giving in to the temptation. Since not everything that we are tempted to do is bad, we must first understand whether what we are being tempted to do is indeed 'evil or sinful'. Many temptation situations are "good things taken to extreme or out of their normal use" before they become actually sinful. To conquer temptations, we need to understand the Biblical guidelines, be totally convinced that this behavior is wrong (and thus needs to be resisted) and identify what our conscience and the Bible is telling us. Lastly, we need to be disciplined and learn how to escape from yielding to the temptation. Temptations to do wrong are the work of the evil one (the devil) and they will be personalized to the areas where we are most vulnerable. The temptation will not necessarily be the same as that experienced by friends or family; but it will be something that somebody else also struggles with. So, we should never feel ashamed about our specific temptation(s); they are "common to humanity" as the Bible says. As we read these verses, take an inventory of your personal vulnerabilities, and design a strategy to deal with it. If it is a tendency to substance abuse (nicotine, alcohol, or recreational drugs), you must be extremely vigilant about what you allow yourself to be exposed to. If its gambling, then don't plan a vacation in a Las Vegas hotel. If its pornography or sex outside of marriage, then watch what you watch and how you conduct yourself around those that you are specifically attracted to. It is important to clearly understand 1 Cor 10:13 below because God promises "a way out". What does that exit route look like for you?

Where do temptations come from? Not from God, rather, they come from the evil one. Temptations follow a sequence called the 'Temptation Triad' - Desire, then Action, followed by Death.

"No one undergoing a trial should say, I am being tempted by God, since God is not tempted by evil, and *he himself doesn't tempt anyone.* But each person is tempted when he is drawn away and enticed by his own evil desire. Then after desire has conceived, it gives birth to sin, and when sin is fully grown, it gives birth to death." - James 1:13-15 CSB

Why does the devil tempt us?

• *The devil's goal is to destroy us, and he does it with lies.*
"A thief comes only to steal and kill and destroy. I have come so that they may have life and have it in abundance." - John 10:10 CSB

• *Temptation to sin is a war against your soul. This is an invisible cosmic battle between Satan and God over each of us.*
"Dear friends, I urge you as strangers and exiles to abstain from sinful desires that wage war against the soul." - 1 Peter 2:11 CSB

• *Temptations will always be there until we die and go to Heaven; therefore, we must not be discouraged about it. Also, do not tempt others.*
"One day, Jesus said to his disciples, There will always be temptations to sin, *but how terrible it will be for the person who does the tempting.*" Luke 17:1, NLT.

What kinds of temptations do we encounter? Always remember that the Bible says your temptations are similar to those of others. You are not alone in this! Although Satan tempts us, God is in ultimate control and will limit the temptations and provide a way out. Always look for the escape route because it is there – take it.

• *Temptations are in common things – money, sex, power, control etc.*
"No temptation has come upon you except what is common to humanity. But God is faithful; he will not allow you to be tempted beyond what you are able, but with the temptation *he will also provide a way out* so that you may be able to bear it." - 1 Corinthians 10:13 CSB

• *Temptations for power and control. In Luke 4 (discussed in detail below) we see Jesus tempted to worship the devil to gain earthly power. Money and power are common temptations for us today.*

• *Temptations to love money – it is one of the key traps of the devil.*
"But those who want to be rich fall into temptation, a trap, and many foolish and harmful desires, which plunge people into ruin and destruction. *For the love of money is a root of all kinds of evil*, and by craving it, some have wandered away from the faith and pierced themselves with many griefs." - 1 Timothy 6:9-10 CSB
Hebrews 13:5

• *Temptation of selfish ambition.*
"Who among you is wise and understanding? By his good conduct he should show that his works are done in the gentleness that comes from wisdom. But if you have bitter envy and selfish ambition in your heart, don't boast and deny the truth. *Such wisdom does not come down from above but is earthly, unspiritual, demonic.* For where there is envy and selfish ambition, there is disorder and every evil practice. But the wisdom from above is first pure, then peace-loving, gentle, compliant, full of mercy and good fruits, unwavering, without pretense. And the fruit of righteousness is sown in peace by those who cultivate peace." - James 3:13-18 CSB

• *Temptation to say inappropriate things. Controlling your tongue is really important and there will be many times you will be tempted to say something inappropriate.*
"For we all stumble in many ways. If anyone does not stumble in what he says, he is mature, able also to control the whole body." - James 3:2 CSB
James 3:1-9, 15

• *Temptations can be incessant—the case of Samson as told in Judges 16. Samson's weakness was sexual addiction. God had given Samson supernatural strength linked to his Nazarite vow. Part of the vow was not to shave his hair.* Delilah was persistent in her temptation to get him to reveal his secret, and Samson did nothing to get away from it. He did not take the way of escape and continued to put himself in a position to be tempted. He enjoyed it, was addicted to it and it cost him his God-given gift and his life. Read the entire chapter of Judges 16.

"*Because she nagged him day after day* and pleaded with him until she wore him out, he told her the whole truth, and said to her, My hair has never been cut because I am a Nazirite to God from birth. *If I am shaved, my strength will leave me, and I will become weak and be like any other man.*" Judges 16:16-17, CSB."

Questions:

1. Why does Peter describe temptations as a war against the "soul"? "Dear friends, I urge you as strangers and exiles to abstain from sinful desires that wage war against the soul." - 1 Peter 2:11 CSB

2. What are the areas where you are most tempted? How are you going to avoid those temptations?

3. Do you notice a variability in temptations? Are there days or even seasons when they do not bother you and then others where it is intense?

4. What are strategies to control your tongue? Or your pen?

5. Can you give an example of the temptation of 'selfish ambition'? How can this be 'unspiritual' and even 'demonic' as James says in 3:15?

Questions with suggested answers:

1. Why does Peter describe temptations as a war against the "soul"? "Dear friends, I urge you as strangers and exiles to abstain from sinful desires that wage war against the soul." - 1 Peter 2:11 CSB

Answer: They are a temptation against "your" soul and thus they are personal not a temptation against a country or team. They are also against the "soul" and not the body. In other words, these temptations impact where you will spend eternity.

2. What are the areas where you are most tempted? How are you going to avoid those temptations?

Answer: This is a personal question that you do not need to necessarily share with others unless you want to. But remember, it's very likely that others are tempted in that area too. Read I Corinthians 10:13 again. Are you looking for the escape hatch?

3. Do you notice a variability in temptations? Are there days or even seasons when they do not bother you and then others where it is intense?

Answer: As Jesus found out, the temptation ended, and the devil walked away. Yes, there will be variability and often the temptations may be the worst when you are walking closely with Jesus. Have you noticed this pattern? Being spiritually very close to God will often make the devil tempt you even more, so be aware.

4. What are strategies to control your tongue? Or your pen?

Answer: The tongue is a wonderful creation very necessary for taste, chewing your food and speaking. The passage in James 3 warns us to use our speech for good and points out how our speech can get us into trouble. In the days before the internet, it was common to send a letter to someone if you were upset or complaining. My Dad always warned us children to not send the letter hastily in a fit of anger. His words were, "write the letter and put it in an envelope and then let it sit there at least overnight before reading again, sealing and sending." Many times, a person will feel differently after a good nights sleep. Today, the immediate nature of Tweets, emails, and phone calls can allow us to say something that cannot easily be "walked back". The passage in James tells us to avoid such temptations.

5. Can you give an example of the temptation of 'selfish ambition'? How can this be 'unspiritual' and even 'demonic' as James says in 3:15?

Answer: The extreme examples of selfish ambition that are frankly demonic and evil are the Nazi rulers (Hitler, Goebbels et al) in World War II. They aimed to make Germany a superior race and power by killing millions. This was a fanatical idea (selfish ambition) of Hitler's. We are seeing this again in 2022 - 24 with the unprovoked attack of Putin in Russia on Ukraine. These rulers are plagued by 'selfish ambition'.

Strategies from the Bible on Dealing with Temptation.

The Bible makes it clear that temptation is common and is to be expected and is part of the devil's plan to destroy us. Even if we lived in a cave or an abbey, the devil would still seek us out. It is a daily battle. But we see here, in the verses below, very useful and practical strategies to deal with temptation.

There are three sets of Biblical strategies detailed below. The first is from Jesus in Luke 4; the second is from Ephesians 6 where Paul describes the Armor of God and the third are miscellaneous verses on the Biblical strategies of physical avoidance (turning away), mental (prayer), and trusting Jesus. In addition to these, Paul recommends in Romans 12 to "do good". *Doing the right thing is a defense against doing the wrong thing.* It also requires vigilance and action as Jesus said, "Get up and pray." Although you may feel overwhelmed at times, remember that the battle is fought on a daily (not yearly) basis, and we can handle anything for a day. Each morning, we get a new allotment of strength from the Lord. Let's look at all the tools that the Bible says are available to you to conquer your temptations starting first with Jesus.

The Temptation of Jesus in Luke 4 – what did Jesus do? He relied on the Holy Spirit and the Word of God to resist. The devil is crafty and used Scripture out of context to tempt Jesus who answered with Scripture. The devil's goal was to destroy Jesus and break up the eternal plan to save the world from sin. The temptations lasted 40 days and occurred at a time when Jesus was weakened physically by being in the wilderness and without food. We learn the importance of the Holy Spirit and Scripture. Jesus's response to each temptation was short and with Scripture. The lesson for us is to always ask, "Is there something in the Bible that will help me respond to this temptation?

• Jesus faced the temptation armed with the Holy Spirit.
"Then Jesus left the Jordan, *full of the Holy Spirit*, and was led by the Spirit in the wilderness for forty days to be tempted by the devil. He ate nothing during those days, and when they were over, he was hungry." - Luke 4:1-2 CSB

• Temptation #1 – the temptation to take matters into your own hands and cease relying on God for your provision (in this case, food). Jesus answers with Scripture from Deuteronomy 8.
"The devil said to him, "If you are the Son of God, tell this stone to become bread." But Jesus answered him, "It is written: Man must not live on bread alone." - Luke 4:3-4 CSB

• Temptation #2 – to worship Satan and gain control of the world. To some extent God has given Satan control over the earth. Satan tempts Jesus to take that earthly power and control by worshiping him.
"So he took him up and showed him all the kingdoms of the world in a moment of time. The devil said to him, I will give you their splendor and all this authority, because it has been given over to me, and I can give it to anyone I want. If you, then, will worship me, all will be yours. And Jesus answered him, It is written: Worship the Lord your God, and serve him only. - Luke 4:5-8 CSB

• Jesus responds with Deuteronomy 6.
"Fear the LORD your God, worship him, and take your oaths in his name."Do not follow other gods, the gods of the peoples around you," - Deuteronomy 6:13-14 CSB

• *Temptation #3 – the Devil uses Scripture from Psalm 91 ("For he will give his angels orders concerning you, to protect you in all your ways. They will support you with their hands so that you will not strike your foot against a stone." - Psalm 91:11-12 CSB) to try and trick Jesus into killing Himself.*

"So he took him to Jerusalem, had him stand on the pinnacle of the temple, and said to him, If you are the Son of God, throw yourself down from here. For it is written: He will give his angels orders concerning you, to protect you, and they will support you with their hands, so that you will not strike your foot against a stone." - Luke 4:9-11 CSB

• *Jesus responds with Scripture*

"And Jesus answered him, It is said: Do not test the Lord your God." - Luke 4:12 CSB.

• *The temptation was temporary, and the Devil ended it. We do not always have control over the duration of temptation.* For example, notice that when Jesus was tempted by the devil as recorded in Matthew 4:1-11 and Luke 4 that the temptation ended only when the devil ended it; *but it did end, and the devil eventually left Him.* Then the devil left him, and angels came and began to serve him." - Matthew 4:11 CSB. The devil is behind temptations, *and they will come and go.*
Luke 4:13

• *Because Jesus conquered this severe temptation, He can be trusted to help you with your temptation! "Every area" includes "your area"!*

"For we do not have a high priest who is unable to sympathize with our weaknesses, but one *who has been tempted in every way as we are, yet without sin.* Therefore, let us approach the throne of grace with boldness, so that we may receive mercy and find grace to help us in time of need." - Hebrews 4:15-16 CSB

The Armor of God - Seven Steps to Conquering Temptation.

In Ephesian's chapter 6, Paul gives valuable tips as to how to battle the temptations of Satan and hardships in life. He uses word pictures of a soldier's armor (called the armor of God) to be used in a spiritual battle. God created the world perfectly, but once sin entered the earth, creation has been in a cosmic battle of Satan (evil, darkness, night) vs God (good, light, day) over our souls. This battle is real, although not always open for others to see in the sense of guns and swords. The Bible is very clear about this and provides clear directions on what to anticipate, how to recognize and how to defend against the attacks of the devil. The battle for our souls may not seem to be fierce and

Satan often works quietly and subtly but Satan is at work. Be wary…do not let your guard down.

Step 1: Keep calm and remember the vast strength of the Lord behind us. Obey the command to 'armor up'! Put all the armor on leaving no areas of vulnerability.

"Finally, be strengthened by the Lord and *by his vast strength. Put on the full armor of God so that you can stand against the schemes of the devil.*" - Ephesians 6:10-11 CSB

"But since we belong to the day, let us *be self-controlled* and put on the armor of faith and love, and a helmet of the hope of salvation." - 1 Thessalonians 5:8 CSB

Step 2: You are in a battle. Who is the enemy? It is the devil.

"For our struggle is not against flesh and blood, but against the rulers, against the authorities, against the cosmic powers of this darkness, against evil, spiritual forces in the heavens." - Ephesians 6:12 CSB

Step 3: Be prepared to stand and resist; notice there is not a command to attack.

"For this reason take up the full armor of God, *so that you may be able to resist* in the evil day, and having prepared everything, to take your stand." - Ephesians 6:13 CSB

"… If you do not stand firm in your faith, then you will not stand at all." - Isaiah 7:9 CSB

Step 4: Use all the tools of the armor of God; you must put them on.

"Stand, therefore, with *truth like a belt* around your waist, right*eousness like armor on your chest*, and your *feet sandaled with readiness for the gospel of peace*. In every situation take up the *shield of faith* with which you can extinguish all the flaming arrows of the evil one. Take the *helmet of salvation* and the *sword of the Spirit* -- which is the word of God." - Ephesians 6:14-17 CSB

• ***Belt represents truth.*** Being truthful…telling the truth…being a trustworthy, truthful person is an important component of the armor. The Roman belt was key to the rest of the armor because the breastplate and the scabbard for the sword were anchored to the belt. *If you are not truthful then the rest of the armor will be flimsy.*

• ***Breastplate of righteousness.*** Do the right thing; be the right person. Righteousness fits nicely with truth.

• ***Footwear – gospel of peace***: the Roman sandal had nails in the soles to allow the soldier to stand firm against the enemy and conquer difficult terrain. The gospel (good news) will lead to peace with God and the person will have the peace of God.

• ***Shield of faith:*** Faith is a key part of the armor because it is easy in the spiritual battle to become weary and fearful and to doubt one's ability to really stand firm against the devil. With faith, we trust that God will keep His promises to help us conquer the temptation or attack. The Roman shield was rectangular (about 2.5 x 4 feet) and covered with leather. It was able to defend against arrows launched by the enemy. The arrows were often on fire to cause more harm. When the soldiers stood side by side and crouched under their shields held together, they created a shield of protection. The "arrows" are temptations or attacks on the Christian. Satan designs the arrows specifically for you and your known weaknesses. Learn to recognize these "arrows" and have your shield of faith. Having friends and being a church fellowship (small group) allows one to meet temptations together and bring the shields together to form a wall. However, choose friends wisely – friends can also tempt us and draw us into temptation.

• ***Helmet of salvation:*** The helmet protects our brain, the command center of our body. This reminds us that our ultimate source of strength in the spiritual battle is to believe Christ's sacrifice for our sin and becoming a Christ-follower.

• ***Sword:*** the Roman sword was double-edged and thus represents in this word picture the Holy Spirit and the Word of God. You must base your defense on the Bible and the help of the Holy Spirit.

Step 5: Prayer: We are to pray in the power of the Holy Spirit. Prayer requires alertness.

"Pray at all times in the Spirit with every prayer and request, and stay alert with all perseverance and intercession for all the saints." - Ephesians 6:18 CSB

Ephesians 6:18-20 CSB

Step 6: Beware of deceivers. They will try to get you to abandon your faith. The Bible uses the word picture "wolves in sheep's clothing".

"Be on your guard against false prophets who come to you in sheep's clothing but inwardly are ravaging wolves." - Matthew 7:15 CSB

Step 7: Discern who the deceivers are by becoming a fruit inspector.

"You'll recognize them by their fruit. Are grapes gathered from thornbushes or figs from thistles? In the same way, every good tree produces good fruit, but a bad tree produces bad fruit. A good tree can't produce bad fruit; neither can a bad tree produce good fruit. Every tree that doesn't produce good fruit is cut down and thrown into the fire. So you'll recognize them by their fruit." - Matthew 7:16-20 CSB

Question with suggested answer:

1. Explain the term "wolves in sheep's clothing". Can you give an example?

Figure 2 – Wolf in Sheep's clothing.

Answer: This is an example of deception. This term was picked up by Aesop who turned it into a short story. The idea in the fable is the same as the Bible tip – watch out for people who pose as good when underneath they are actually evil.

> "A Wolf found great difficulty in getting at the sheep owing to the
> vigilance of the shepherd and his dogs. But one day it found the skin

of a sheep that had been flayed and thrown aside, so it put it on over its own pelt and strolled down among the sheep. The Lamb that belonged to the sheep, whose skin the Wolf was wearing, began to follow the Wolf in the Sheep's clothing; so, leading the Lamb a little apart, he soon made a meal off her, and for some time he succeeded in deceiving the sheep, and enjoying hearty meals. Appearances are deceptive. Aesop's Fable

Additional Biblical strategies to deal with temptation.

Take mental action to resist temptation.

• Don't plan or think about ways to satisfy the temptation. Do not purposely get close to the temptation where we can get sucked in. This is walking on the proverbial "slippery slope".
"Instead, clothe yourself with the presence of the Lord Jesus Christ. *And don't let yourself think about ways to indulge your evil desires.*" - Romans 13:14 NLT

• Think eternal as Moses did—he could have enjoyed the sin but rather he looked ahead to eternity and said— "eternity is worth more than earthly pleasure". It is important to note here that Moses admitted the sin was indeed pleasurable. It usually is for a "fleeting moment". That is not the point. It's that the activity is sinful, and he saw through that to eternity.

"By faith Moses, when he had grown up, refused to be known as the son of Pharaoh's daughter. He chose to be mistreated along with the people of God rather than to enjoy the fleeting pleasures of sin. He regarded disgrace for the sake of Christ as of greater value than the treasures of Egypt, because he was looking ahead to his reward." - Hebrews 11:24-26 NIV

• Play dead to sin—die to it—we are to consider ourselves dead to this temptation. Dead people do not commit sin.
"So, you too consider yourselves dead to sin and alive to God in Christ Jesus." - Romans 6:11 CSB
Romans 6:11-14, Colossians 3:5, Colossians 3:8-10

• **Be done with old habits of sin. Follow God's instructions to the Israelites regarding old idols. If they are not destroyed, they will hang around and tempt us again.**
"*Burn up the carved images of their gods.* Don't covet the silver and gold on the images and take it for yourself, *or else you will be ensnared by it,* for it is detestable to the LORD your God." - Deuteronomy 7:25 CSB

• **Trust Christ for the victory. Jesus is a reliable coach because He has "been tempted and won the battle".**
"For every child of God defeats this evil world by *trusting Christ to give the victory.* And the ones who win this battle against the world are the ones who believe that Jesus is the Son of God." 1 John 5:4, 5, NLT.

Hebrews 2:17, 18, NLT.

• **Aim for holiness – "be holy".**
"But as the one who called you is holy, you also are to be holy in all your conduct; for it is written, Be holy, because I am holy." - 1 Peter 1:15-16 CSB

"Therefore, with your minds ready for action, be sober-minded and set your hope 1 Peter 1:13-16 CSB

Physical action to resist the temptation to do wrong.

• **Doing good things will take our mind off doing evil things.**
"Do not be conquered by evil, but conquer evil with good." - Romans 12:21 CSB

• **Use the "three aways".** When Joseph in the Bible was tempted to have sex with the boss's wife, he used this strategy – keep out of the way; turn away; run away.

• **Keep out of the way of the temptation – use Avoidance.**
"And Potiphar's wife soon began to look at him lustfully. Come and sleep with me," she demanded. ... She kept putting pressure on Joseph day after day, but he refused to sleep with her, and *he kept out of her way as much as possible.*" - Genesis 39:7, 10 NLT

"Dear children, *keep away from anything that might take God's place in your hearts.*" - 1 John 5:21 NLT

• *Turn away if it cannot be avoided.*

"One day, however, no one else was around when he went in to do his work. She came and grabbed him by his cloak, demanding, Come on, sleep with me! *Joseph tore himself away*, but he left his cloak in her hand as he ran from the house." - Genesis 39:11-12 NLT

My child, if sinners entice you, *turn your back on them*!" Proverbs 1:10, NLT.

• *Run away – if all fails – run.*

"Although she spoke to Joseph day after day, he refused to go to bed with her. Now one day he went into the house to do his work, and none of the household servants were there. She grabbed him by his garment and said, "Sleep with me!" *But leaving his garment in her hand, he escaped and ran outside.* When she saw that he had left his garment with her and had run outside," - Genesis 39:10-13 CSB

The words of Charles Spurgeon, the great English preacher of the 19th century, summarizes Joseph's action best "The wings of a dove may be of more use to me today than the jaws of a lion…better to leave my cloak than my character…it is not needful that I be rich but it is imperative upon me to be pure."

Prayer

• *Jesus in His final days told His disciples to pray to avoid temptation.*

"He went out and made his way as usual to the Mount of Olives, and the disciples followed him. When he reached the place, he told them, *Pray that you may not fall into temptation.*" - Luke 22:39-40 CSB

"Why are you sleeping? " he asked them." *Get up and pray*, so that you won't fall into temptation." - Luke 22:46 CSB

• *The Disciple's Prayer – recite this short prayer from Jesus that includes the topic of temptation.*
Matthew 6:9-13, KJV."

Spiritual growth - keep growing in your faith and build up your defenses.

• *Take the advice of Peter.* "His divine power has given us everything required for life and godliness through the knowledge of him who called us by his own glory and goodness. *By these he has given us very great and precious promises, so that through them you may share in the divine nature, escaping the corruption that is in the world because of evil desire.* For this very reason, *make every effort to supplement your faith with goodness, goodness with knowledge, knowledge with self-control, self-control with endurance, endurance with godliness, godliness with brotherly affection, and brotherly affection with love.* For if you possess these qualities in increasing measure, they will keep you from being useless or unfruitful in the knowledge of our Lord Jesus Christ. The person who lacks these things is blind and shortsighted and has forgotten the cleansing from his past sins. *Therefore, brothers and sisters, make every effort to confirm your calling and election, because if you do these things you will never stumble."* - 2 Peter 1:3-10 CSB

Help others who are being tempted.

• *We can help others, but we must do it with humility and care.*
"Dear brothers and sisters, if another Christian is overcome by some sin, you who are godly, should gently and humbly help that person back onto the right path. And be careful not to fall into the same temptation yourself." Galatians 6:1, NLT.

Summary: These are clear strategies for resisting temptations. They are: Put on the Armor of God as discussed above. Actively do good things (mental). Never plan to sin and avoid situations that would place you near it. Pray to God for help; help others; and be dead to sin and alive to God. Lastly, be like Moses and look beyond the momentary pleasure of earthly sin to eternal pleasure in Heaven.

Questions:

1. Identify the temptations that you are vulnerable to. Are you convinced they are wrong? What does the Bible say about this activity?

2. In the story of Joseph and Potiphar's wife, was it brave or cowardly for Joseph to run away from the situation?

3. How do you help others with temptations without getting tainted ('getting burned') yourself? Can you think of examples of Galatians 6:1?

4. What Paul mean in Romans 6:11 about being "dead to sin"?

5. Why is sin usually temporarily pleasurable? Hebrews 11:24-26.

6. Read the Hansei Cronje story about temptation.

7. What are the results of resisting temptation?

Questions with suggested answers:

1. Identify the temptations that you are vulnerable to. Are you convinced they are wrong? What does the Bible say about this activity?

Answer: This is a personal question that first requires taking an inventory of the temptations that bother you. Typically, it will be something inherently good taken to an evil extreme. For example, if it is sexual activity – that is good and normal within the marriage relationship but sinful outside of marriage. In order to tackle the temptation and use the strategies above you have to be convinced it is indeed sinful. This is important in addictions such as alcohol – many people with alcohol problems think that their use is ok and that they can "take a little drink" without being overcome. Their road to recovery is realizing the problem and the severity of it.

2. In the story of Joseph and Potiphar's wife, was it brave or cowardly for Joseph to run away from the situation?

Answer: Joseph tried avoidance and turning away but he was in a situation of being an Egyptian slave and could not merely quit his job. So, in the end he had to run rather than give into Potiphar's wife. Sometimes to avoid temptation you have to leave your friends and run rather than be involved.

3. How do you help others with temptations without getting tainted ('getting burned') yourself? Can you think of examples of Galatians 6:1?

Answer: If you want to help someone, make sure you bring others and watch yourself. If you previously had this problem and conquered it, you may be called to work with others to help them. But sometimes it will make you vulnerable again.

4. What Paul mean in Romans 6:11 about being "dead to sin"?

Answer: "So, you too consider yourselves *dead to sin and alive to God* in Christ Jesus." - Romans 6:11 CSB. This means that once we become a believer in Jesus and are given the Holy Spirit we are under no obligation to give in to temptation and sin. Paul clarifies this later in Romans 12:1-2 "Therefore, brothers and sisters, in view of the mercies of God, I urge you to present your bodies as a living sacrifice, holy and pleasing to God; this is your true worship. Do not be conformed to this age, but be transformed by the renewing of your mind, so that you may discern what is the good, pleasing, and perfect will of God." When a suffering person dies we say there pain is over and they are at peace. So it is with sin – when we die to it we stop being controlled by it and we live a new life for Christ.

5. Why is sin usually temporarily pleasurable? Hebrews 11:24-26.

Answer: These are extremely important verses, and they demonstrate how true the Bible is and that it totally understands the reality of temptations. "By faith Moses, when he had grown up, refused to be called the son of Pharaoh's daughter and chose to suffer with the people of God rather than to enjoy the fleeting pleasure of sin. For he considered reproach for the sake of Christ to be greater wealth than the treasures of Egypt, since he was looking ahead to the reward." - Hebrews 11:24-26 CSB

Moses loved living in the palace of the Pharaoh. Who would not? It was pleasurable. Almost every sin – sexual, racing at high speeds, drug addictions, power, money, and gambling are all associated with a momentary "high" that is truly pleasurable followed by a quick return to earth and the reality of what we just did. Having casual sex is enticing and pleasurable but for a very short time and then the emotional (and physical sometimes) damage is done that can last a lifetime. Getting drunk may feel great for bit but then the hangover sets in. Moses had faith and he looked forward to eternity and this gave him the power and strength to avoid the temptations.

6. Read the Hansei Cronje story about temptation.

Answer: Hansei Cronje was the captain of the South African cricket team in the 1990's. He was a Christian and revered by many in society for his skills on the field, his good looks, his wife and family and his leadership abilities. Unfortunately, as the movie *"Journey to Grace: The Hansie Cronje Story 2008 Netflix* depicts, he was enticed multiple times by bookmakers from India who paid him money to influence the outcome of the cricket games (matches). Although he never actually purposely did anything illegal on the field, he did accept money from them and was banned from cricket. His downfall was sudden and complete. If you actually watched the movie, you will have noted how Satan, through the bookies, used a strategy of persistent, low-level temptation over time. Satan initially approached him with lies and innocent requests. By not dealing immediately with the temptation ("killing it") he instead "toyed with it" and eventually fell for it through rationalization. In the end he found forgiveness and restoration through Jesus and his church.

So, if God forgives the sin, why is it such a big deal? Some sins, although forgiven, leave the person permanently scarred for life as we see in Hansei. He lost his livelihood, and he suffered emotional distress. If the sin is criminal, the person may go to prison or be ineligible for certain jobs. It can ruin marriages and have lifelong effects on children. Can you think of other cases where the person fell into temptation, caused harm to others, and suffered long term consequences despite being forgiven?

7. What are the results of resisting temptation?

Answer: A sense of victory, a clean conscience, and close communion with God who helped you through it. However, it's not always all roses. Your "friends" who may have been encouraging you to participate in a sinful (or potentially sinful) activity, may ridicule you for not joining. Remember this verse from Peter "For there has already been enough time spent in doing what the Gentiles choose to do: carrying on in unrestrained behavior, evil desires, drunkenness, orgies, carousing, and lawless idolatry. They are surprised that you don't join them in the same flood of wild living -- *and they slander you*. They will give an account to the one who stands ready to judge the living and the dead." - 1 Peter 4:3-5 CSB.

Thomas Witzig

4

What is a Biblical Marriage?
What is Biblical Sex?

Marriage and sexual activity are designed by God and indeed the Bible has much to say on both of these topics. Although there are many books written about sex, in *this book*, *in this chapter,* the discussion is limited to what the Bible says. This is because the reader should be most interested in hearing what the Designer of sex says about it rather than some friend, internet site, newspaper, popular public figure, this author, or even a professional sex counselor. Sex was designed by God to be between a man and a woman within a Biblical marriage. There are several purposes of sex as described in the Bible. The two most obvious are - sexual pleasure between the couple and having children (procreation). Yes, God fully understands the pleasure of marital sex - He designed it that way. However, sex, like fire, must be used properly or else it will damage people. Pay attention especially to what Solomon writes in the books of *Proverbs* and *Song of Solomon*. Solomon writes from vast sexual experience. The Bible says in 1 Kings 11 that he had over 300 concubines and these women turned him away from God and led to his downfall. In the end, after all those physical sexual experiences, he recommends monogamy! Sadly, he learned the hard way and we should heed his warnings.

Remember that the sexual language used in the Bible is also a powerful spiritual metaphor. This means that the writer is using sexual language as an analogy. For example, in the Old Testament God describes His love for Israel and in the New Testament Jesus and the universal Church are described as bridegroom and bride (a marriage metaphor). Then there is the beautiful *Song of Solomon*, a very sexual book with a much higher meaning about how Jesus loves us so dearly, but again not in a sexual way. Lastly, in Revelations 18 Babylon the Great is described as having committed sexual immorality with other kings, a word picture of worldliness.

In medical school before diseases of an organ are studied, professors spend considerable time teaching the normal function of that organ. Only after the student understands what is normal can the pathologies (diseases) be understood and studied. The same applies to sex - we need to understand God's original design and what we will refer to as "Biblical sex" and "Biblical marriage" so as to clearly remind the reader that we are using Biblical definitions. These teachings also provide an explanation of the Bible's use of sexual intimacy as a metaphor of love and desire for a relationship with God.

What is Biblical Marriage? How is marriage defined in the Bible? What is the normal Biblical standard?

The original design as described in the book of Genesis was the separate creation of males and females with Adam being created first, then Eve. They were made to be compatible ("fit") for each other anatomically and emotionally. The aim of the marriage relationship was to "leave and cleave" as described in the original KJV translation of Genesis 2:24."Leave" meant separation from each birth family and "cleave" meant to develop a bond so special that a husband and wife in this new union live as "one". This "leave and cleave" concept - to separate from parents and bond to each other - is symbolized by the physical act of sexual intercourse. In the marriage relationship there is no shame in sexual activity between the man and the woman.

• *Biblical marriage is between a genetic XY male and a genetic XX female. This was defined early in Genesis.*
"The man gave names to all the livestock, to the birds of the sky, and to every wild animal; but for the man no helper was found corresponding to him. So the LORD God caused a deep sleep to come over the man, and he slept. God took one of his ribs and closed the flesh at that place. Then the LORD God made the rib he had taken from the man into a woman and brought her to the man. And the man said: This one, at last, is bone of my bone and flesh of my flesh; this one will be called "woman," for she was taken from man. *This is why a man leaves his father and mother and bonds with his wife, and they become one flesh.* Both the man and his wife were naked, *yet felt no shame*." - Genesis 2:20-25 CSB

• *Jesus confirmed Biblical marriage in the New Testament.*
Mark 10:6-10, CSB."

• *Biblical marriage is designed to be lifelong - "until death do us part".*
"A wife is bound as long as her husband is living. But if her husband dies, she is free to be married to anyone she wants — only in the Lord. But she is happier if she remains as she is, in my opinion. And I think that I also have the Spirit of God." - 1 Corinthians 7:39-40 CSB"

• *Jesus said that Biblical marriage occurs on earth but not in heaven.*
"For when they rise from the dead, they neither marry nor are given in marriage but are like angels in heaven." - Mark 12:25 CSB

• *Biblical marriage is honorable, designed by God, and monogamous sex is the plan.*
Monogamy is the standard from the time of Genesis, and it was to be special and long-lasting. Multiple partners are not Biblical marriage because they defile the "marriage bed" and relegate sex to a mere physical act.

"This is why a man leaves his father and mother and bonds with *his wife*, and they become one flesh." - Genesis 2:24 CSB

Genesis 2:24 KJV

"Some Pharisees approached him to test him. They asked, Is it lawful for a man to divorce his wife on any grounds? Haven't you read, he replied, that he who created them in the beginning made them male and female, and he also said, For this reason a man will leave his father and mother and be joined to his wife, and the two will become one flesh? So they are no longer two, but one flesh. Therefore, what God has joined together, let no one separate." - Matthew 19:3-6 CSB

• *Biblical marriage is characterized by honor and respect for each other.* The couple recognize the physical and emotional differences between them and build on them. Notice the key words "honor", "coheirs" while recognizing the physical strength may (but not always) differ.

"Husbands, in the same way, live with your wives in an understanding way, as with a weaker partner, showing them honor as coheirs of the grace of life, so that your prayers will not be hindered." - 1 Peter 3:7 CSB

• *Biblical marriage is characterized by a deep love for each other – the example of Isaac and Rebekah. Notice how Rebekah was a comfort to Isaac.*

"And Isaac brought Rebekah into his mother Sarah's tent, and she became his wife. *He loved her deeply, and she was a special comfort to him after the death of his mother.*" - Genesis 24:67 NLT

In summary, Biblical marriage is to be between a genetic male and genetic female; it is to be monogamous (one of each not one man with multiple females), mutually satisfying, honorable, loving, and lifelong.

Question with suggested answer:

1. What is the difference between Biblical marriage and marriage as currently defined in the United States or a civil union as defined in some countries?

Answer: After reading the verses in the Bible it is clear what God intended marriage to be. That is why we call it "Biblical marriage". As noted below in **Figure 3**, the closer we as people or a society are to God and the more we value His Book the Bible, the more likely our *legal laws* will match our *moral code* as described in the Bible. That is why for years no one argued for same-sex marriage (the marriage between two people of the same genetic sex). This idea was initially voted down but then eventually it became law in the US. So, now same sex unions are considered legal marriage. This misses the definition of marriage as defined in the Bible. Many churches will not conduct these unions as marriage because of the definition of Biblical marriage.

God

Legal Code

Moral Code

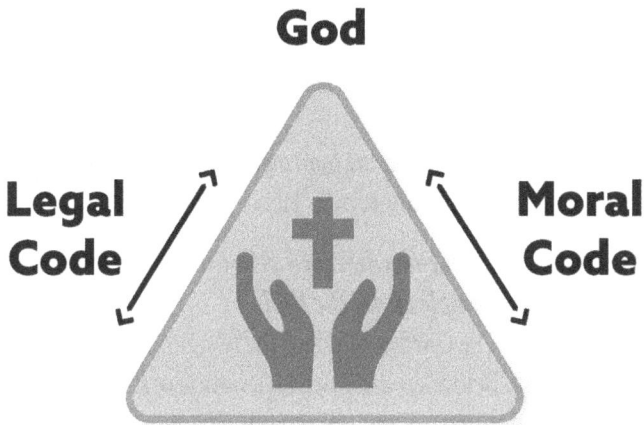

Figure 3: The closer we are to God the more likely the legal codes established in our government and courts will match the moral codes from the Bible. As society devalues God, our moral codes mean less and hence the laws change. We all suffer the results.

Sexual drive and intimacy in Biblical marriage. Sex within marriage has two purposes: (A) mutual pleasure that produces physical and emotional bonding between the man and wife (the leave and cleave concept) and (B) reproduction (having children). In addition to Genesis, the prophet Malachi also writes of this key Biblical marriage concept of "one flesh" and "reproduction" and reminds the man to respect and value his wife. Two translations of this verse are provided below. The word translated "treacherously" is the Hebrew *bagad* and indeed it does mean treacherous or deceitful.

"Didn't God *make them one* and give them a portion of spirit? What is the one seeking? Godly offspring. *So watch yourselves carefully, so that no one acts treacherously against the wife of his youth.*" - Malachi 2:15 CSB
Malachi 2:15

• *Sexual intercourse and drive are a "profound mystery" and are to be understood within its higher metaphorical meaning.*
"For this reason, a man will leave his father and mother and be joined to his wife, and the two will become one flesh. *This mystery is profound*, but I am talking about Christ

and the church. *To sum up, each one of you is to love his wife as himself*, and the wife is to respect her husband." - Ephesians 5:31-33 CSB

• *Sexual activity within marriage is God's design and honorable. It is the Biblical plan and is sacred.*
"Marriage is to be honored by all *and the marriage bed kept undefiled*, because God will judge the sexually immoral and adulterers." - Hebrews 13:4 CSB

• *Sexual activity within marriage was designed to be beautiful and not embarrassing or shameful. Here are some examples from the Bible.*

> **• *Adam and Eve.*** The Garden of Eden, the first home of Adam and Eve did not require clothing. Before sin there was no emotion of shame and thus the natural tendency to cover ourselves was not present. Shame over the exposure of private body parts (your genitalia or sex organs) comes when sin enters the world.

"Both the man and his wife were naked, *yet felt no shame.*" - Genesis 2:25 CSB

> **• Boaz and Ruth.** Their story shows that sexual intimacy is normal and right within marriage. This is also called, "making love". It is love that is key to this act - love and physical pleasure are entwined in Biblical sex. The physical attraction is important. Notice that Boaz first married Ruth then the sexual activity occurred. The other byproduct of sex is children.

"Boaz took Ruth and she became his wife. *He slept with her*, and the LORD granted conception to her, and she gave birth to a son." - Ruth 4:13 CSB

"So Boaz took Ruth and she became his wife. *When he made love to her*, the LORD enabled her to conceive, and she gave birth to a son." - Ruth 4:13 NIV

> **• Jacob and Rachel.** Sexual attraction is real, normal, mysterious, and meant to be enjoyed. It is part of "loving your spouse".

"Now Laban had two daughters: the older was named Leah, and the younger was named Rachel. Leah had tender eyes, *but Rachel was shapely and beautiful. Jacob loved Rachel*, so he answered Laban, I'll work for you seven years for your younger daughter Rachel." - Genesis 29:16-18 CSB

• *Jacob was sexually attracted to Rachel. It is normal that he was not looking at marriage to just produce children. Jacob desired sexual intimacy, but he knew he needed to be married first.*

"Then Jacob said to Laban, Since my time is complete, *give me my wife, so I can sleep with her.*" - Genesis 29:21 CSB

> • *Solomon.* He talks about sexual pleasure with the "wife of your youth". Note the enduring pleasure of sexual intimacy (physical and emotional touch) throughout years of marriage ("forever").

"Drink water from your own cistern, water flowing from your own well. ... Let your fountain be blessed, and *take pleasure in the wife of your youth.* A loving deer, a graceful doe -- let her breasts always satisfy you; *be lost in her love forever.*" - Proverbs 5:15, 18-19 CSB

• *A husband and wife are a team and need to satisfy the needs of each other. Paul recommended a healthy, mutually satisfying sex life as defined by the marriage couple.* The sexual needs will differ in frequency and desire; the keys are mutual satisfaction and loving; never abusive or forced. These are general guidelines – thus, defined by the couple and not some textbook or manual. The Bible acknowledges that withholding sex within marriage is potentially dangerous and can be used by the devil.

"A husband should fulfill his marital duty to his wife, and likewise a wife to her husband. A wife does not have the right over her own body, but her husband does. In the same way, a husband does not have the right over his own body, but his wife does. Do not deprive one another -- except when you agree for a time, to devote yourselves to prayer. Then come together again; otherwise, Satan may tempt you because of your lack of self-control. I say this as a concession, not as a command." - 1 Corinthians 7:3-6 CSB

Summary of Normal Biblical Sex and Marriage (Table 1): Biblical marriage is designed by God and dates to the very beginning of the Bible in Genesis 2. It is clearly defined in the Bible as between one man and one woman. God designed it to be very enjoyable when kept sacred in the marriage. It is to be characterized as a new family unit that establishes a new home. Marital sex fulfills the physical and emotional sexual drive and bonds the man and woman together. The sex drive is important to maintain closeness especially in the early years of the marriage. It is also built in to lead to procreation. This picture of marriage between a man and woman is also a powerful metaphor in Scripture as Jesus Christ the Bridegroom and the Church as the Bride.

Table 1: Normal sexual activity within a Biblical marriage as described in the Bible.

Type	Description
Metaphorical Meaning of Sexual Activity	The word picture of the sexual relationship as our love for Jesus as illustrated by the Church (Bride) and Jesus (the Bridegroom).
Optimal Sexual Activity	Bonding of husband and wife in an emotional and physical union of one flesh that has an element of mystery. The ideal; does not always occur.
Sex for procreation	In the younger years of marriage, the goal of sexual intercourse may be to conceive and bear children.
Sex for pure pleasure	Emotional and physical activity (with or without climax) that meets the overall physical and emotional needs of each partner in a Biblical marriage. This type of sexual activity spans the lifetime of the marriage and thus is not necessarily designed for procreation.

Questions:

1. Does the Bible provide sexual counseling regarding techniques and how to deal with physical and emotional problems with sex that can come within a marriage?

2. Is it normal to wait until marriage to have sexual intercourse? Is that the design?

3. Why does the Bible say that marital sex is a "mystery"?

4. Why does Paul tell men in Ephesians 5:31 "To sum up, each one of you is to love his wife as himself, and the wife is to respect her husband."?

Questions with suggested answers:

1. Does the Bible provide sexual counseling regarding techniques and how to deal with physical and emotional problems with sex that can come within a marriage?

Answer: Thankfully, it does not. The Bible lays out the key principles – that sexual activity is important, normal, and to be enjoyed within a monogamous marriage between a man and a woman. Remember not to define marital sexual intimacy as only intercourse – it then becomes an all or nothing act. There can be much satisfaction in marriage around physical and emotional touch. Although sex may consume a relatively small amount of time in the life of the couple, it is a key part of marriage, and is to be enjoyed without guilt. It also has a deep spiritual meaning that couples do not always treasure or think about. Christians are not and should not be prudish about sex within Biblical marriage; they are however instructed to keep sex within the marriage. *How a couple meets the sexual needs of each other is between them and that also is beautiful.* Learning and meeting your spouse's needs in this area is a life-long part of marriage. Most people do not share these intimate details with friends, family, or their children. As a couple traverses the years of marriage from newlyweds to the childbearing years to the mature years without children, the sexual needs may change. Again, this is up to the couple to work out. Of course, if there are problems they should be addressed by medical professionals and counselors. An excellent book that many (including my wife and I) have found helpful is *The 5 Love Languages- The Secret to Love that Lasts* by Gary Chapman.

2. Is it normal to wait until marriage to have sexual intercourse? Is that the design?

Answer: Yes, that is the Biblical design and recommendation. Sex before marriage is of course physically enjoyable in the moment. However, this uncouples the link between the physical and emotional/bonding aspects of sexual intercourse. The result is an episode of short physical pleasure without enduring emotion or bonding. If the episode was merely designed as a "hook-up" or if the relationship breaks up and marriage does not ensue, there can be an emotional hangover where the memories of the experience(s) linger and can interfere with intimacy in the future. Lastly, these transient physical acts miss the higher-level meaning of sex that God designed and risk the spread of diseases that can have long-term implications for when you actually choose your mate and attempt childbearing. Remember, nobody (even the Bible) denies that sex is pleasurable, it just needs to be kept sacred in the marriage. Sex without the emotional, marital bond is just "transient physical sexual pleasure".

3. Why does the Bible say that marital sex is a "mystery"?

Answer: The Ephesians 5 passage is speaking mainly about the use of sexual intercourse as a metaphor of the church as the Bride of Christ. However, sexual drive can be hard to fully understand even though you have been married to your spouse for many years. This mystery of love and sexual desire makes lovemaking in its broadest sense with your spouse enjoyable for years.

4. Why does Paul tell men in Ephesians 5:31 "To sum up, each one of you is to love his wife as himself, and the wife is to respect her husband."?

Answer: This is a short verse with a lot of practical meaning. On the surface it may seem odd to talk about self-love, but this is referring I believe for the man to have healthy self-esteem and value. A man that knows who he is in God's eyes and is content with that and is not ashamed of himself will be motivated to be kind and loving towards his wife. Embedded in this is also the second greatest commandment "The second is, Love your neighbor as yourself. There is no other command greater than these." - Mark 12:31 CSB. In order for the woman to be a good partner, she must respect her husband otherwise it will be difficult for her to bond and love him and make the marriage successful.

How does the evil one disrupt the Biblical Plan for Biblical sex?

Now that we understand the definition of Biblical marriage and Biblical sex, we can move on to what the Bible says about the distortions of the original plan. Satan is always trying to disrupt the normal designs and purposes of God. After sin entered the world (referred to as the Fall) in Genesis 3, the plan for Biblical sex became distorted. The devil usually takes things that are good to an extreme or out of bounds where the situation becomes sinful. *Therefore, the Bible sets the boundaries of acceptable sexual relations in humans.* The Bible defines the behaviors and acts that are sinful and criminal providing the basis for what our society defines today as "sex crimes". Our judicial system in the United States defines *criminal* sex acts largely on the Biblical standards. However, in recent years, the judicial code has changed to redefine some sex acts as "not criminal" even though they are not following the Biblical standards. That is why the Biblical "moral code" is sometimes different than the "criminal code" and these criminal codes vary by state and by country. When discussing these issues in the classroom or public it is important to remember – is this activity legal? If legal, is it moral or immoral (wrong) in God's eyes? In summary, according to the Bible, God designed sex to be between husband and wife within marriage, and if misused people are harmed. The Bible is not shy about any of this. In addition, we are given some useful strategies to keep sexual activity in its proper perspective. *Because sex is such a powerful natural and physical drive it is one of the most common temptations that Satan will use to trip you up.*

What are the consequences of the original sin to the sexual relationship?

• *Guilt and shame.* After Adam and Eve sin and become aware of it, they feel guilt and shame over their nakedness. The result is painful labor in childbirth for Eve, stress in marriage, and farming becomes difficult for Adam due to weeds and pests. The man and woman begin to cover their private parts (genitalia) because of the shame. To provide the clothing (covering) they need animal skins (leather); thus, we observe the first mention of blood sacrifice.

"Then the man and his wife heard the sound of the LORD God walking in the garden at the time of the evening breeze, and *they hid from the LORD God* among the trees of the garden. ... Then he asked, Who told you that you were naked? Did you eat from the tree that I commanded you not to eat from? ... He said to the woman: I will intensify your labor pains; *you will bear children with painful effort.* Your desire will be for your husband, yet he will rule over you. And he said to the man, Because you listened to your wife and ate from the tree about which I commanded you, 'Do not eat from it': The *ground is cursed because of you.* You will eat from it by means of painful labor all the days of your life. ... The *LORD God made clothing from skins for the man and his wife, and he clothed them.* ... So the LORD God sent him away from the garden of Eden to work the ground from which he was taken." - Genesis 3:8, 11, 16-17, 21, 23 CSB

• *Painful childbirth and a distorted marital relationship.* This punishment includes conflict and disruption of the normal sexual relationship in marriage. This started with Adam and Eve after they both sinned.

"He said to the woman: I will intensify your labor pains; you will bear children with painful effort. Your desire will be for your husband, yet he will rule over you." - Genesis 3:16 CSB

• *Sex can also become disconnected with marital love.* The true goal of Biblical marriage is that sexual intimacy in all its forms be connected to love for one's spouse. But sex can become disconnected from love and become just a physical act. In the case of

Leah in Genesis 29 it was obvious that she was having sex with her husband Jacob and indeed children were being born but she still felt unloved. She longed for more than just the physical part of sex – she wanted emotional attachment to her husband. This case speaks to the two-pronged purpose of sex. Sex for the purpose of only procreation, misses the love. Sex for physical pleasure only can also become loveless and very transient. This case is also one of the first examples of polygamy (a man having more than one wife) and the problems it brings.

"Leah conceived, gave birth to a son, and named him Reuben, for she said, The LORD has seen my affliction; *surely my husband will love me now.* She conceived again, gave birth to a son, and said, *The LORD heard that I am unloved* and has given me this son also. So she named him Simeon. She conceived again, gave birth to a son, and said, "*At last, my husband will become attached to me* because I have borne three sons for him." Therefore he was named Levi." - Genesis 29:32-34 CSB

What are the Biblical boundaries of sex?

• *Sexual activity is to occur within Biblical marriage.* Sex was and is part of God's design. It is normal, but like all normal functions it has boundaries and *sex was designed to be kept within marriage.*

"Now in response to the matters you wrote about: "*It is good for a man not to use a woman for sex.*" But because sexual immorality is so common, *each man should have sexual relations with his own wife,* and *each woman should have sexual relations with her own husband.*" - 1 Corinthians 7:1-2 CSB

Note the high respect of women and how Paul says they are not to be "used for sex". Only the CSB translation of this verse says "not to use"; most translations say "touch". The Greek word used here is *hapto* which means to bind or attach to or kindle a fire. In medicine, the prefix hapto means to attach. Haptoglobin is a protein that attaches to hemoglobin. In this Bible verse the point is "don't attach yourself to a woman merely for sex". Why? Because it is physical only without the love.

• *Sexual acts outside of marriage are considered "sexual immorality" and are outside the boundaries of acceptable Biblical sex.* Sexual immorality is a work of the flesh. The Greek word for immorality is *porneia,* a broad term that encompasses all the sexual sins in and outside of Biblical marriage. The word used in the passage below for moral impurity is *akatharsia*, which means being impure or unclean.

"Now the works of the flesh are obvious: sexual immorality, moral impurity, promiscuity, idolatry, sorcery, hatreds, strife, jealousy, outbursts of anger, selfish ambitions, dissensions, factions, envy, drunkenness, carousing, and anything similar. I am warning you about these things -- as I warned you before -- that those who practice such things will not inherit the kingdom of God." - Galatians 5:19-21 CSB

• *Understand that sexual sin is a result of the flesh nature not the Spirit.*
"I say then, walk by the Spirit and you will certainly not carry out the desire of the flesh. For the flesh desires what is against the Spirit, and the Spirit desires what is against the flesh; these are opposed to each other, so that you don't do what you want." - Galatians 5:16-17 CSB

What sexual activities are considered morally wrong (sinful) as defined by the Bible? Given that Biblical sex is normal and desirable as defined above, what can go wrong? Who can get hurt? This beautiful sexual relationship designed by God became subject to degradation by the Fall (the sin of Adam and Eve in the Garden of Eden) and we see the results of this in society today. In all these sexual sins, sexual activity is reduced to merely physical pleasure. In some sins the physical pleasure is mutual and consensual (agreement between two parties without it being in writing). In the criminal acts the pleasure is one sided and forced and not in agreement with one of the persons.

The sexual pathologies are defined here (Table 2 below) using Biblical definitions. Some of these sins are also considered criminal in the United States and variably around the world. The verses supporting the definitions follow. Note that the terms "Biblical definitions" and "sexual sins as defined by the Bible" are used to clearly differentiate these from the personal opinions of others, your classmates or teachers, those found on the Internet or social media, in the newspaper or television or the workplace. We will all someday answer to God for the way we lived our lives. It is safest to live by Biblical guidelines.

As we begin to discuss this important, but rather sensitive area, we need to remember 3 key facts:

(A) Sexual sins are but one of many sins outlined in the Bible. They are important but should not be overemphasized. Notice how many other common sins are listed alongside sexual sins in this Romans 1 passage.
Romans 1:28-32

(B) Sexual sins are different because they are a sin against our own bodies. They also involve other people who will also suffer long-lasting bodily and emotional harm. Your body is a temple of the Holy Spirit; do not misuse it. We were not made for sexual sin. This is not the way God designed sex to be.

"Flee sexual immorality! Every other sin a person commits is outside the body, but the person who is sexually immoral sins against his own body. *Don't you know that your body is a temple of the Holy Spirit who is in you, whom you have from God?* You are not your own, for you were bought at a price. So glorify God with your body." - 1 Corinthians 6:18-20 CSB

1 Corinthians 6:12-17 CSB

(C) Sexual sins can be forgiven and be overcome. Note how the verse below notes how people became changed after becoming a Christ follower.

"Don't you know that the unrighteous will not inherit God's kingdom? Do not be deceived: No sexually immoral people, idolaters, adulterers, or males who have sex with males, no thieves, greedy people, drunkards, verbally abusive people, or swindlers will inherit God's kingdom. And some of you used to be like this. *But you were washed, you were sanctified, you were justified in the name of the Lord Jesus Christ and by the Spirit of our God.*" - 1 Corinthians 6:9-11 CSB

Table 2: Types and levels of sexual activity as defined as pathologic (wrong, harmful) in the Bible. A sex act may be morally wrong (sinful per Bible guidelines) yet not criminal under civil law. All criminal acts as defined in the United States are currently also considered sinful or morally wrong.

Pathological Sexual Activity As Defined Using Bible Standards

Moral vs Legal	Frequency	Activity
Sinful as defined Biblically; *not criminal* in the United States.	Common	Lust – coveting another person for sexual purposes in your mind. This is moving beyond mere attraction or 'first look' into the sin of coveting another person for sexual pleasure.
		Adultery – consensual heterosexual physical sexual *acts* (not just inclination or temptation only) with a person outside the marriage.
		Fornication – consensual heterosexual physical sexual *acts* (not just inclination or temptation only) between unmarried people.
		Adultery and fornication encompass most of what is referred to as "casual sex" or "hook-ups" or "one-night stands". It is sex for physical pleasure only. It is the end-product of lust as described above.
Sinful as defined Biblically; *not criminal* in the US	Uncommon	Consensual homosexual sexual *activity* (not just inclination or temptation only) between those of the same sex.
Sinful as defined Biblically; criminal in the US.	Common	Sexual immorality – pornography; prostitution (real or virtual); sexual harassment including unwanted sexual speech and physical touching.
Sinful and criminal in the US	Rare	Rape – unwanted sexual activity of any type - homosexual or heterosexual. Sex with children (pedophilia). Polygamy (multiple spouses).
Sinful and criminal in the US	Extremely rare	Sex with animals (sodomy); Sex with family members (incest).

Lust - the sin of coveting sexual activity. The beginning of all sexual sins.

Lust is a common sexual sin identified and discussed in the Bible. It is not considered legally wrong (criminal) because it is mostly unseen and in the mind of the individual. Jesus talked about it because He knew that it was the first step in what leads to sexual immorality and eventually sexual intercourse outside of marriage (adultery). *Lust is a desire for transient physical sex only, not the enduring emotional bonding and intimacy that characterizes Biblical marriage.* Lust can also apply to other strong desires such as for money, power, and control. Lust is a form of coveting – wanting something too much and that something belongs to another. Let's look at some of the key verses from the Bible then circle back to discuss this important sin.

• *Looking and lusting (not just looking) is the first step towards the physical act. Jesus warned of the seriousness of contemplating adultery.*

"But I tell you, everyone who looks at a woman lustfully has already committed adultery with her in his heart." - Matthew 5:28 CSB

• *Solomon said - Lust occurs in the heart and mind.*

"They will protect you from an evil woman, from the flattering tongue of a wayward woman. *Don't lust in your heart for her beauty or let her captivate you with her eyelashes."* - Proverbs 6:24-25 CSB

• *Lust can be heterosexual or homosexual – both acts are sinful.*

"The men in the same way also left natural relations with women and were *inflamed in their lust* for one another. Men committed *shameless acts* with men and received in their own persons the appropriate penalty of their error." - Romans 1:27 CSB

• *Lust is usually the initial temptation; then, if perpetuated it leads to sin. Temptation, then lust, then action, then sin and death. This is a progression, and it is best to deal with it and stop it at the temptation stage.*

"No one undergoing a trial should say, I am being tempted by God, since God is not tempted by evil, and *he himself doesn't tempt anyone.* But each person is tempted when he is drawn away and enticed by his own evil desire. Then after desire has conceived, it gives birth to sin, and when sin is fully grown, it gives birth to death." - James 1:13-15 CSB

• *If you feel lust, it is never from God, rather it is from your sin nature.*
"For everything in the world -- the lust of the flesh, the lust of the eyes, and the pride in one's possessions -- *is not from the Father*, but is from the world." - 1 John 2:16 CSB

• *Lust will vanish in Heaven – this is very encouraging.*
"And the *world with its lust is passing away*, but the one who does the will of God remains forever." - 1 John 2:17 CSB

• *Do not covet and that includes another person.* The Hebrew word for covet is *chamad* which means to desire or covet or lust. This is a warning to not overly desire what is not ours. The sin of coveting or lusting is very general as the verse gives several examples. There is nothing wrong with admiration or wanting something; coveting is taking it to the extreme and like many good things in life when they are taken too far it turns negative or something bad happens like adultery, divorce, stealing etc.

"Do not covet your neighbor's house. Do not covet your neighbor's wife, his male or female servant, his ox or donkey, or anything that belongs to your neighbor." - Exodus 20:17 CSB

• *The end result of unchecked lust can allow our natural sin nature to "take its course" resulting in sex acts and sexual perversion.* Worshipping sex for the physical act itself will result in all kinds of sexual sin and sexual acts. Romans 1:18-25 CSB

Summary: Lust is a very tricky sin because it is usually hidden in the brain of a person. *Lust is the seed that if not controlled can sprout and develop into in all kinds of sexual sins.* Jesus understood this because He called lust for another woman to be equivalent to adultery. By describing it as a male lusting after another woman Jesus also understood that this problem is especially difficult for men. This is not to be confused with sexual attraction or noticing that a person is attractive (in your eyes) as they walk by in the workplace or appear in a video/movie. A person cannot help the "first look" but returning to "gaze or stare repeatedly" leads to the beginning of a physical desire that can turn into lust (see James 1:13-15 above).

Perhaps a non-sexual example here will help to understand this situation. When I see pictures of Mt Everest, I admire the beauty and majesty of the snow-covered mountain peaks, but I am not in the least bit tempted to join an expedition to climb that mountain. Admiration? yes; lust? no. Attractive woman? Yes, I certainly admit that she is beautiful but not for me and I move on! For most men sexual lust will be an issue in certain phases of life and perhaps their entire adult life. Men do not typically talk about this but if they do it is clear that what they are lusting for is the momentary physical pleasure of the sex act rather than a desire for a long-lasting marital bond with the person. There is definitely a biological hormonal aspect to sexual attraction that accounts in part for the problem of lust. Loss of the male hormone testosterone or the female hormone estrogen as adults age or undergo medical procedures can alter the problem of lust.

The sin of adultery – sexual intercourse with a partner outside of your marriage.

The mysterious sex drive, when used properly within Biblical marriage, is important to the health and richness of marriage. However, like all good things when it is misused it leads to pathologies, dysfunction, hurt and sometimes overt criminal activity. These are clearly defined in the Bible just as normal Biblical sex is defined. These passages may be difficult to read, especially the ones in the Old Testament but they are necessary to clearly prove that the Bible considers adultery a moral sin. Adultery is common and in the United States is usually not considered criminal. In some states fines can be levied. Adultery is often depicted in the movies, in novels and on TV. In fact, you may have observed it and its consequences in your own immediate or extended family. How did it turn out after the short exhilaration of the act? What were the long-term consequences?

• Adultery is a major sin – the seventh of the Ten Commandments. It is major because it fractures the marriage bond of trust and spoils the special relationship between a man and woman.
"Do not commit adultery." - Exodus 20:14 CSB

• Jesus clearly reaffirms #7 of the Ten Commandments and takes it a step further by telling us mental adultery (lust) is the precursor state (the first stage) before the physical act of adultery. He also states that this problem starts with the eyes which are of course the lens into your "heart" or visual cortex. The brain integrates that signal and makes choices regarding what it will do with that signal. Nobody but you and God know about your mental adultery. However, if you are successful at stopping it there, it will not lead to the physical act.

"You have heard that it was said, Do not commit adultery. But I tell you, everyone who looks at a woman lustfully has already committed adultery with her in his heart." - Matthew 5:27-28 CSB

Matthew 5:29-30

• *Adultery with another man's wife can lead to big problems beyond the sin itself.* It is destructive and disgraceful. In the movies it is often depicted as exciting and pleasurable but that is only momentary. If it occurs in the workplace, you lose your job.

"*The one who commits adultery lacks sense; whoever does so destroys himself.* He will get a beating and dishonor, and his *disgrace will never be removed.* For jealousy enrages a husband, and he will show no mercy when he takes revenge. He will not be appeased by anything or be persuaded by lavish bribes." - Proverbs 6:32-35 CSB

• *The metaphor of the sexual sin of adultery – "You will get burned".*
"They will protect you from an evil woman, from the flattering tongue of a wayward woman. Don't lust in your heart for her beauty or let her captivate you with her eyelashes. ... *Can a man embrace fire and his clothes not be burned? Can a man walk on burning coals without scorching his feet? So it is with the one who sleeps with another man's wife; no one who touches her will go unpunished."* - Proverbs 6:24-25, 27-29 CSB

• *Adultery leads to secondary sins.* King David's adultery with Bathsheba is a classic case of adultery and its consequences. David's adultery led to murder and the death of a child. Note the steps that David took in leading to sin. The first look, followed by inquiry, then invitation, and then the sin occurs.

"In the spring when kings march out to war, David sent Joab with his officers and all Israel. They destroyed the Ammonites and besieged Rabbah, but David remained in Jerusalem. One evening David got up from his bed and strolled around on the roof of the palace. From the roof he saw a woman bathing -- a very beautiful woman. So David sent someone to inquire about her, and he said, "Isn't this Bathsheba, daughter of Eliam and wife of Uriah the Hethite? David sent messengers to get her, and *when she came to him, he slept with her.* Now she had just been purifying herself from her uncleanness. Afterward, she returned home. The woman conceived and sent word to inform David: I am pregnant." - 2 Samuel 11:1-5 CSB

• *Sex with another man's wife/concubine/possession was considered 'wrongdoing' in the Old Testament. This goes beyond adultery to sexual activity between unmarried people.*
2 Samuel 3:7-8 CSB

• These sins were so disgusting to God that He regretted making humankind. Sexual sin led to the Universal Flood and a reduction in age to 120 years.
- Genesis 6:1-7 CSB

"When the LORD saw that human wickedness was widespread on the earth and that every inclination of the human mind was nothing but evil all the time, the LORD regretted that he had made man on the earth, and he was deeply grieved. Then the LORD said, "I will wipe mankind, whom I created, off the face of the earth, together with the animals, creatures that crawl, and birds of the sky -- for I regret that I made them." - Genesis 6:5-7 CSB

• People who commit adultery will experience judgement.
"Marriage is to be honored by all and the marriage bed kept undefiled, because God will judge the sexually immoral and adulterers." - Hebrews 13:4 CSB

Questions:

1. Why is adultery such a seductive sin? Why is it often portrayed in movies as normal and exciting.

2. Your mother dies in a car accident. Several years go by and your father informs you that he plans to marry a woman who also lost her spouse to cancer. Is this marriage permitted by God? After they are married is sexual activity considered adultery because it is not with their original spouses?

3. Adultery and fornication can lead to more than just emotional distress and the breakdown of relationships. There are also physical consequences. Can you name some?

Questions with suggested answers:

1. Why is adultery such a seductive sin? Why is it often portrayed in movies as normal and exciting.

Answer: The sexual drive can be very strong and sexual activity from enticement to intercourse is very pleasurable. But God designed the act to be more than just physical and emotional pleasure – it is a part of the very important intimate bond and trust between a man and a woman. Because it is so pleasurable the devil uses it as one of his top strategies to entice people to sin. The very idea that it is such an important bond in the marriage means that when that trust is broken and there is adultery in the marriage there are many consequences. Sometimes the adultery leads to lying and to other sins (see the case of King David). In September 2022 Ime Ndoka Head Coach of the Boston Celtics was suspended for committing adultery with a woman on the Celtics staff. The activity was consensual (meaning it was not criminal). Why did the Celtics do this? Not so much because they were concerned about breaking God's law but rather because adultery or any sexual activity between a boss and a subordinate is considered wrong. Notice the fallout – Ndoka loses his high-profile job (and money) and he also causes major disruption with the relationship with his fiancée.

2. Your mother dies in a car accident. Several years go by and your father informs you that he plans to marry a woman who also lost her spouse to cancer. Is this marriage permitted by God? After they are married, is sexual activity considered adultery because it is not with their original spouses?

Answer: Remarriage after death of a spouse is clearly permitted. Marriage is until death.

"A wife is bound as long as her husband is living. But if her husband dies, she is free to be married to anyone she wants — only in the Lord. But she is happier if she remains as she is, in my opinion. And I think that I also have the Spirit of God." - 1 Corinthians 7:39-40 CSB

3. Adultery and fornication can lead to more than just emotional distress and the breakdown of relationships. There are also physical consequences. Can you name some?

Answer: We refer to these as STDs (sexually transmitted diseases). The bacterial ones associated with sexual intercourse are gonorrhea and syphilis. Viral diseases such as the HIV can also be spread this way. The movie "Contagion" (released well before COVID-19) describes a worldwide viral pandemic in which a female executive on a business trip, contracts the disease in a casino in Hong Kong then gives it to another friend with whom she has a hook-up in Chicago during an airplane layover. This is a case of adultery against her husband, and it costs her and the adulterer their lives. Although this movie is fiction it illustrates the lure of sexual hook-ups followed by physical consequences. The best prevention of STDs is to have sex only with your marriage partner. As of January 2023, the organism *Neisseria gonorrhoeae* has acquired resistance to all routine antibiotics and remains dangerous.

The sin of homosexual sex acts. In the Bible (especially the Old Testament) there are many passages that describe the details and results of sexual activity outside of Biblical marriage, summarized in Table 2. These range from adultery to sexual acts outside of the marriage relationship when a person is not married, to taking of other women into the household for sexual pleasure (concubines), prostitution (sex for money or other favors), same sex acts (homosexual acts), and sex with family members (incest). Most sinful sexual activity is between members of the opposite sex, but occasionally it can be between members of the same sex. This is known as same-sex (homosexual) sexual activity. All these sexual sins (both heterosexual and homosexual) stray far from the standard of Biblical marriage and Biblical sexual activity as described above. These sexual acts occur because they are indeed short-lived physical and emotional sexual pleasures and if not resisted, they will occur. This is what Paul refers to in Romans 1 when he writes about letting your body follow its sexual desires without any guidelines. In the New Testament the instructions are clear to avoid sexual immorality, but the descriptions are less graphic and perhaps easier to discuss openly in a class or small group. It is important to note that in the verses below it is always the sexual act itself that is the sin not just feelings or attraction.

• *Homosexual acts, like heterosexual acts outside of marriage are considered wrong in the Old Testament.* They are discussed early in the Bible in the book of Genesis; therefore, these are not new types of sexual sin.

    • The case of Sodom and Gomorrah two cities in the area of Israel.

"Before they went to bed, the men of the city of Sodom, both young and old, the whole population, surrounded the house. They called out to Lot and said, "Where are the men who came to you tonight? Send them out to us so we can have sex with them! " Lot went out to them at the entrance and shut the door behind him. He said, "*Don't do this evil,* my brothers." - Genesis 19:4-7 CSB

"Likewise, Sodom and Gomorrah and the surrounding towns *committed sexual immorality and perversions,* and serve as an example by undergoing the punishment of eternal fire." - Jude 1:7 CSB

"You are not to sleep with a man as with a woman; *it is detestable.*" - Leviticus 18:22 CSB

2 Peter 2:4, 6, 9

• The Case of the men of Gibeah.

They were considered wicked to desire homosexual acts and the acts were described as evil – Judges 19:16-23.

• *Same sex activity occurs in both men and women.* These activities are acknowledged to occur then and now, and the Bible does not ignore them. In the Bible they are described as unnatural and shameful. They involve lust for physical pleasure and the participants basically worship the sexual experience. This was part of the curse at the time of the sin of Adam and Eve – shame was part of it.
Romans 1:24-28

• *These sexual acts are one of many potential sins we can fall into.*
Romans 1:28-32

• *Sexual sins can be forgiven – notice verse 11 – "but you are no longer like that".*
"Don't you know that the unrighteous will not inherit God's kingdom? Do not be deceived: No sexually immoral people, idolaters, adulterers, or males who have sex with males, no thieves, greedy people, drunkards, verbally abusive people, or swindlers will inherit God's kingdom. And some of you used to be like this. But you were washed, you were sanctified, you were justified in the name of the Lord Jesus Christ and by the Spirit of our God." - 1 Corinthians 6:9-11 CSB

• *We are to move past former sins committed before we believed in Jesus.*
"Therefore, preparing your minds for action, and being sober-minded, set your hope fully on the grace that will be brought to you at the revelation of Jesus Christ. *As obedient children, do not be conformed to the passions of your former ignorance*, but as he who called you is holy, you also be holy in all your conduct," - 1 Peter 1:13-15 ESV

Summary: Unnatural sexual activity as described in the Bible includes both heterosexual and homosexual sex acts. Just like heterosexual *attraction* is not sin per se neither is homosexual *attraction*. Attraction for sinful things is part of human nature…it's the action and lust that are the sins. That is an important distinction. Also, remember that we are not to single out one sin and overemphasize it. Paul lists a whole lot of sins in verses 28-32; I am certain the reader can identify with many of these. Lastly, these sexual sins can be forgiven – the 1 Corinthian 6 passage is encouraging.

Questions:

1. Why did Jesus focus on the sin of lust?

2. Is there a difference in a sexual sin if it is committed by a Christ-follower rather than a person who is an unbeliever?

Questions with suggested answers:

1. Why did Jesus focus on the sin of lust?

Answer: He understood that sexual sins start in the mind and that is the place to stop them. This is critical to conquering any of these sins. Lust goes beyond sex – it can be a lust for power, for money for anything.

2. Is there a difference in a sexual sin if it is committed by a Christ-follower rather than a person who is an unbeliever?

Answer: There would be no difference in the treatment of the person if the sex sin was criminal. If it is not a criminal sex sin then yes, the consequences could be different. Unbelievers do not have the Holy Spirit and thus will thus be guided by their feelings and emotions and physical attractions. Sexual pleasure is one of the highest forms of pleasure and very difficult to resist if allowed to proceed. If an unbeliever is living in a situation where sexual activity is involved, then we focus on bringing that person into a knowledge of the Bible and trust that God will convict them of their sin after a conversion experience happens. If the person is a committed Christian and is openly committing sexual sin (or any other open sin), then this will need to be dealt with by the church to help the person(s) repent and turn from the sin.

The sin of prostitution.

Prostitution is selling (for money or other compensation) one's body (male or female) for the sexual pleasure of another person. This is described in the Bible and is considered sinful. There are two aspects to the Bible's description of prostitution, and these must be understood as one reads Bible passages on this subject. First, prostitution is a physical and sexual sin that is common in many societies. Secondly, since the Bible metaphorically likens the marital relationship to Christ as the bridegroom and we the Church as the bride, some passages refer to "spiritual prostitution". Spiritual prostitution is the sin of leaving Jehovah God for an idol and this is considered spiritual adultery and is also a sin. For example, Ezekiel 23 is not about two actual women with sordid pasts; rather, it is a word picture of the nation Israel and its unfaithfulness to God. *This must be understood as one reads these passages or you will be totally confused.* In the US, prostitution is criminal in all 50 states except for several counties in Nevada. It is a degrading practice to all partners and completely misses the purpose of sex in marriage and turns it into transient physical pleasure. The effects on the mind and the sexually transmitted diseases are well described in the medical literature and the Bible.

• The Greek word *pornos* is used in the New Testament and translated into English as 'sexually immoral'. *Pornos* refers to use of the body in prostitution (male or female).
"But the cowards, faithless, detestable, murderers, sexually immoral, sorcerers, idolaters, and all liars -- their share will be in the lake that burns with fire and sulfur, which is the second death." - Revelation 21:8 CSB

• Letting a daughter be a prostitute or facilitating it was sinful. Notice how the sin of prostitution also affects the whole country or culture.
"Do not debase your daughter by making her a prostitute, *or the land will be prostituted and filled with depravity*." - Leviticus 19:29 CSB

• The sexual sin of prostitution leads to idolatry and weakness of the Nation.
"While Israel was staying in the Acacia Grove, *the people began to prostitute themselves with the women of Moab.* The women invited them to the sacrifices for their gods, and the people ate and bowed in worship to their gods. *So Israel aligned itself with Baal of Peor, and the LORD's anger burned against Israel.* The LORD said to Moses, "Take all the leaders of the people and execute them in broad daylight before the LORD so that his burning anger may turn away from Israel. So Moses told Israel's judges, Kill each of the men who aligned themselves with Baal of Peor." - Numbers 25:1-5 CSB

• Solomon acknowledges the transient pleasure of being with a prostitute but warns against the long-term consequences and shame at the end of his life. The description of physical consequences speaks to the well-known consequences of sexually transmitted diseases such as gonorrhea, human immunodeficiency virus (HIV), syphilis, and human papilloma virus (HPV). Notice the strategy of avoidance – "don't go near".
Proverbs 5:1-14

• The sordid story of Judah and prostitution in Genesis 38. Judah is tricked by Tamar and falls into the sin. It demonstrates how degraded society was by then.

• Rahab – the most famous prostitute (Hebrew zana which means harlot) in the Bible. She hid the spies in return for a promise that her family would be spared. Joshua 2:1, 8-9, 12-16 CSB She is listed in the Hebrews Hall of Faith Hebrews 11:31 CSB

• Samson's downfall was sex. It all started with prostitution.
"Samson went to Gaza, *where he saw a prostitute and went to bed with her.*" - Judges 16:1 CSB

• Sexual favors can be used to tempt and deceive and lead to destruction. This is the origin of the term "hidden agenda".
"A woman came to meet him dressed like a prostitute, *having a hidden agenda.*" - Proverbs 7:10 CSB

"For a prostitute is a deep pit, and a wayward woman is a narrow well; " - Proverbs 23:27 CSB

• Prostitution was also a symbol or word picture or metaphor for turning away from God to idols or other religions. God refers to it as "breaking a covenant". Why did God use prostitution as an illustration of spiritual betrayal? Because everyone understood it. Prostitution fractures the marriage covenant just like worshipping idols does to our relationship with God.

"These will serve as tassels for you to look at, so that you may remember all the LORD's commands and obey them *and not prostitute yourselves by following your own heart and your own eyes.*" - Numbers 15:39 CSB

"The LORD said to Moses, "You are about to rest with your fathers, and these people will soon *prostitute themselves with the foreign gods* of the land they are entering. They will abandon me and break the covenant I have made with them." - Deuteronomy 31:16 CSB

• The story of Oholah and Oholibah in Ezekiel 23 is all metaphorical. They are a symbolic of the kingdom of Israel (the ten tribes in the north) and the kingdom of Judah (the two tribes in the south). It's a way of describing the spiritual adultery of Israel.

Ezekiel 23:4-5, 35 CSB

The key to these verses is that adultery whether in actual marriage or our spiritual relationship breaks apart our relationship with God leading to terrible consequences.

Question with suggested answer:

1. Why is Rahab's story encouraging?

Answer: It shows that God cares and can use anyone in His work. Secondly, she was able to overcome her past and be mentioned in the Hebrews Faith Hall of Fame (chapter 11). Read a complete summary of her story in Lockyer's *All The Women Of The Bible* https://www.biblegateway.com/resources/all-women-bible/Rahab (accessed April 30, 2021).

The sins of rape and incest.
Rape and incest are evil, very degrading sins. They are the result of a severely depraved mind. Rape is sexual activity that is forced upon a person without their consent. Rape can be heterosexual or homosexual. Incest is when the sexual activity occurs within family members. Rape is always condemned in the Bible and is recognized as a felony crime in the US and in most countries of the world. Incest is a crime in many states, with variable levels of punishment.

• *Rape – the case of Dinah.* Rape was a crime in the Bible and to be punished. Dinah's brothers took the law into their own hands.

"Leah's daughter Dinah, whom Leah bore to Jacob, went out to see some of the young women of the area. When Shechem -- son of Hamor the Hivite, who was the region's chieftain -- saw her, he took her and raped her." - Genesis 34:1-2 CSB

"Jacob's sons returned from the field when they heard about the incident and were deeply grieved and very angry. *For Shechem had committed an outrage against Israel by raping Jacob's daughter, and such a thing should not be done.* ... But Jacob's sons answered Shechem and his father Hamor deceitfully because he had defiled their sister Dinah. ... They killed Hamor and his son Shechem with their swords, took Dinah from Shechem's house, and went away. Jacob's sons came to the slaughter and plundered the city because their sister had been defiled. ... But they answered, "Should he treat our sister like a prostitute?" - Genesis 34:7, 13, 26-27, 31 CSB

• *Rape and incest – the case of Tamar by Amnon.* This is a sad story of incest and rape that led to the death of Amnon. It illustrates that rape was dishonorable in that culture; virginity was respected; rape was avenged. The additional fact that it was an incestuous affair shows how this was considered wrong too.

2 Samuel 13:1, 11-14 CSB

• *Incest – the Case of Reuben.* He defiled himself with the rape of his stepmother.

"Reuben, you are my firstborn, my strength and the firstfruits of my virility, excelling in prominence, excelling in power. Turbulent as water, you will not excel, because you got into your father's bed and you defiled it -- he got into my bed." - Genesis 49:3-4 CSB

Biblical strategies to remain morally and spiritually clean.

As the Bible details, sexual activity was designed to be pleasurable within Biblical marriage. However, anything pleasurable can become sinful if it gets out of control. Fire is a relevant analogy - a fire in the fireplace on a cold Minnesota night is a wonderful and necessary pleasure. However, if the sparks fly out and ignite a nearby stack of paper it may burn the house down. Imagine sexual activity as a meter – normal is desire that is fulfilled in Biblical marriage. Too little sexual activity can be detrimental in a marriage and has a chilling effect. Too much sexual drive leads to sexual addiction and the sexual pathologies described above.

The sexual temptations are very common, and a tool regularly used by Satan. There is a biological hormonal component that drives sexual desire in men and women and thus these temptations are more relevant in the years between the onset of puberty until male and female menopause. This is not an excuse; rather, it is a reality that we live with. The sexual temptations vary between people and are generally worse for men than women given their tendency to be more easily stimulated visually. The temptations are also often situational in that certain people may come into one's life that are extremely attractive and create sexual tension. Because Satan uses sex as a primary way to bring people down and tear marriages apart, he will often use this tool more on Christian men and women than others. *The Bible does not leave us helpless against these temptations.*

All people, married or unmarried, need to develop a strategy to avoid sexual temptations as they are so common in our society. The strategies are:

1. If married, develop and maintain a mutually satisfying sex life with your spouse.

2. Have a high view of your body and marriage. Specifically, men should have a high view of women.

3. Consider sexual sin to indeed be sin – call it what it is.

4. Avoidance of people or any situation that feeds this temptation.

5. Stopping the temptation early at the level of the mind (lust).

6. Combine 1-5 with wisdom and good old-fashioned discipline.

The following verses provide the Biblical support of these strategies.

1. If married, focus on developing a satisfying sex life within Biblical marriage.
Marry the right person and develop a great marriage that prioritizes a healthy sex life that satisfies each other. See the recommendations in Proverbs 5.

"Drink water from your own well--*share your love only with your wife.* Why spill the water of your springs in the streets, having sex with just anyone? You should reserve it for yourselves. Never share it with strangers. *Let your wife be a fountain of blessing for you. Rejoice in the wife of your youth. She is a loving deer, a graceful doe.* Let her breasts satisfy you always. May you always be captivated by her love. Why be captivated, my son, by an immoral woman, or fondle the breasts of a promiscuous woman? For the LORD sees clearly what a man does, examining every path he takes. An evil man is held captive by his own sins; they are ropes that catch and hold him. He will die for lack of self-control; he will be lost because of his great foolishness." - Proverbs 5:15-23 NLT

2. Have a high view of your body. Focus on inner beauty rather than appearance.
Your body is the temple of the Holy Spirit and not your own. An important aspect of developing and maintaining a healthy sex life is to have a high view of your body and the body of your spouse. Men are to have a high view of women and never use them for sex.

"Don't you know that *your body is a temple of the Holy Spirit* who is in you, whom you have from God? You are not your own, for you were bought at a price. So glorify God with your body." - 1 Corinthians 6:19-20 CSB

"Now in response to the matters you wrote about: "It is good for a man not to use a woman for sex." - 1 Corinthians 7:1 CSB

This is also the teaching of the Old Testament book of Song of Solomon which describes the strong link between sex and love. *The adversary tries to separate sex from love thus leading to sex as only a short-term physical pleasure and risking it becoming sinful.* Jesus paid a high price to save you – so glorify God with your body and do not degrade it with sexual sin.

"Don't let your beauty consist of outward things like elaborate hairstyles and wearing gold jewelry, but rather what is inside the heart -- the imperishable quality of a gentle and quiet spirit, which is of great worth in God's sight." - 1 Peter 3:3-4 CSB

3. Consider sexual sin a sin. Just because it feels good does not make it right. Never fall for a short-term pleasure that will destroy a long-term (eternal) reward.

"By faith Moses, when he had grown up, refused to be called the son of Pharaoh's daughter and chose to suffer with the people of God rather than to enjoy the fleeting pleasure of sin. *For he considered reproach for the sake of Christ to be greater wealth than the treasures of Egypt, since he was looking ahead to the reward.*" - Hebrews 11:24-26 CSB

• *Followers of Jesus should avoid sexual immorality*. This was the message that the apostles gave to the early church members in the Book of Acts. It shows that the Church has held these values from the earliest time.

"Therefore, in my judgment, we should not cause difficulties for those among the Gentiles who turn to God, but instead we should write to them to *abstain* from things polluted by idols, *from sexual immorality*, from eating anything that has been strangled, and from blood. ... For it was the Holy Spirit's decision -- and ours -- not to place further burdens on you beyond these requirements: that you *abstain from* food offered to idols, from blood, from eating anything that has been strangled, and from *sexual immorality*. You will do well if you *keep yourselves from these things*. Farewell." - Acts 15:19-20, 28-29 CSB

4. Avoidance – don't put yourself in a situation that induces temptation.

• *Avoidance may require running away*.
"*Flee sexual immorality*! Every other sin a person commits is outside the body, but the person who is *sexually immoral sins against his own body*." - 1 Corinthians 6:18 CSB

• *Run from sin and run towards the good things. Doing good is a great strategy to avoid doing wrong.*
"But you, man of God, *flee from these things, and pursue righteousness*, godliness, faith, love, endurance, and gentleness." - 1 Timothy 6:11 CSB

• *The Case of Joseph in Genesis.* Sexual temptation is not new to our times. The story of Joseph is very informative and occurs in Genesis thousands of years ago. Joseph viewed sexual sin in his case as a 'sin against God' because the woman in the story was willing to have sex. Joseph is unmarried and handsome; however, he views sexual sin outside of marriage as evil and a sin against God. *He considers it evil to her husband but takes an even higher view and sees it as a sin against God.* In the end he runs. He does not toy with the sin; he does not try to talk himself out of the situation nor does he lead her or himself on. He has great willpower. Here is the story.

> • Joseph is Potiphar's house manager. He was trusted. He was handsome. You cannot help it if you are attractive to other people.
> Genesis 39:4-6 CSB
>
> • Potiphar's wife tries to seduce him. Joseph refuses for several reasons – it would betray the master Potiphar since she was his wife and he was trusted; and it, the affair, would be an immense evil and a sin against God. Notice that he does not say that he is not interested in sexual pleasure.
> Genesis 39:7-9 CSB
>
> • The temptation was daily. At this point he could not escape. He simply had to refuse. Since he was a prisoner in Egypt he could not "quit and get another job".
> "Although she spoke to Joseph day after day, *he refused to go to bed with her.*" - Genesis 39:10 CSB
>
> • The day of the attack. No witnesses. This time she grabbed him. More than just a request.
> "Now one day he went into the house to do his work, and none of the household servants were there. She grabbed him by his garment and said, Sleep with me! But leaving his garment in her hand, he escaped and ran outside." - Genesis 39:11-12 CSB
>
> • He runs. She retains part of his clothes.
> Genesis 39:13-18 CSB
>
> • Joseph goes to prison falsely accused but his integrity intact.
> "When his master heard the story his wife told him -- "These are the things your slave did to me" -- he was furious and had him thrown into prison, where the

king's prisoners were confined. So Joseph was there in prison." - Genesis 39:19-20 CSB

This case study of Joseph illustrates key strategies to avoid sexual temptation – recognize the sinfulness of the activity to both parties and to God and be ready to literally leave the situation in a hurry. The Bible has many other strategies for temptation in general and sexual temptations specifically. If sexual temptation is a significant area of weakness, then it will take implementation of all of these strategies for you to win this battle.

Question with suggested answer:

1. The case of Joseph was essentially sexual harassment in the workplace. We hear of these cases often today when people in management are fired because they had sexual relations with people beneath them. We know why the Bible says this is wrong (it is sexual immorality since it is outside Biblical marriage and violates the 7th Commandment in Exodus 20:14) but why would a commercial business care?

Answer: Many of these cases are abusive to the person in the subordinate position. In other cases, the sexual activity is consensual, but the subordinate uses the sexual favors as a means to unfairly obtain a pay raise or a promotion. Allowing this to go on is considered morally wrong by most businesses and many cases of people (mostly men but women too) getting fired can be found in the news.

5. Stop the temptation early before it matures into sin.

• *Wake up – this is a 'big deal'; put on the armor of light; walk decently.*
"Besides this, since you know the time, it is already the hour for you to wake up from sleep, because now our salvation is nearer than when we first believed. The night is nearly over, and the day is near; so let us *discard the deeds of darkness and put on the armor of light*. Let us walk with decency, as in the daytime: not in carousing and drunkenness; not in sexual impurity and promiscuity; not in quarreling and jealousy. But put on the Lord Jesus Christ, and *don't make plans to gratify the desires of the flesh*." - Romans 13:11-14 CSB

• *Learn to recognize when you are being seduced – the hunting analogy of falling into the trap of sexual temptation.*
"She seduces him with her persistent pleading; she lures with her flattering talk. He follows her impulsively like an ox going to the slaughter, like a deer bounding toward a

trap until an arrow pierces its liver, like a bird darting into a snare -- he doesn't know it will cost him his life." - Proverbs 7:21-23 CSB

• *Nip the temptation in the bud - at the level of the mind.*

Jesus said in the passage from Mark quoted below to focus on your heart and mind – "it's what comes out that counts". This is an important concept. One cannot always control what comes across your visual field. Billy Graham, the evangelist who preached in the 20th century, once said regarding temptation, "You cannot prevent a bird from landing on your head, but you can keep it from building a nest there". The point is, acting on the temptation is the key. The word for sexual immorality in the passage from Mark 7 below is 'porneia' which means any form of sexual sin – adultery, fornication, prostitution, pornography etc.

"The Jews, especially the Pharisees, do not eat until they have poured water over their cupped hands, as required by their ancient traditions. ... Then Jesus called to the crowd to come and hear." *All of you listen, he said, and try to understand. It's not what goes into your body that defiles you; you are defiled by what comes from your heart.* Then Jesus went into a house to get away from the crowd, and his disciples asked him what he meant by the parable he had just used. Don't you understand either? he asked.Can't you see that the food you put into your body cannot defile you? Food doesn't go into your heart, but only passes through the stomach and then goes into the sewer. (By saying this, he declared that every kind of food is acceptable in God's eyes.) And then he added, It is what comes from inside that defiles you. For from within, out of a person's heart, come evil thoughts, sexual immorality, theft, murder, adultery, greed, wickedness, deceit, lustful desires, envy, slander, pride, and foolishness. All these vile things come from within; they are what defile you." - Mark 7:3, 14-23 NLT

"Then Peter said to Jesus, Explain to us the parable that says people aren't defiled by what they eat. Don't you understand yet? Jesus asked. Anything you eat passes through the stomach and then goes into the sewer. But the words you speak come from the heart--that's what defiles you. For from the heart come evil thoughts, murder, adultery, all sexual immorality, theft, lying, and slander. These are what defile you. Eating with unwashed hands will never defile you." - Matthew 15:15-20 NLT

• *Obey the warning signs.*

"Now, sons, listen to me, and pay attention to the words from my mouth. Don't let your heart turn aside to her ways; don't stray onto her paths. For she has brought many down to death; her victims are countless. Her house is the road to Sheol, descending to the chambers of death." - Proverbs 7:24-27 CSB

• *Don't stare. You cannot always help the first look, but you can resist the second and third look or the prolonged gaze.* Follow Job's strategy. He knew because he had dealt with it. He had to make a covenant with his eyes. He knew that sexual temptation started in the mind. The eye was the gateway. He also realized the power of this sin – "it would wipe out everything".

"I have made a covenant with my eyes. How then could I look at a young woman? For what portion would I have from God above, or what inheritance from the Almighty on high? Doesn't disaster come to the unjust and misfortune to evildoers? Does he not see my ways and number all my steps? " - Job 31:1-4 CSB

"For *lust is a shameful sin*, a crime that should be punished. It is a fire that burns all the way to hell. *It would wipe out everything I own.*" - Job 31:11-12 NLT

6. Combine 1-5 with wisdom and good old-fashioned discipline.
• *Be wise –Use reminders to avoid sexual sin.*
"*Love wisdom like a sister*; make insight a beloved member of your family. Let them protect you "My son, obey my words, and treasure my commands. Keep my commands and live, and guard my instructions as you would the pupil of your eye. Tie them to your fingers; write them on the tablet of your heart. Say to wisdom, "You are my sister," and call understanding your relative. She will keep you from a forbidden woman, a wayward woman with her flattering talk." - Proverbs 7:1-5 CSB
Numbers 15:37-40

• *Be disciplined.*
  • *Sexual sins will indeed get us all tangled up and lead to death.*"Discipline, not just desire, determines a man's destiny" Roland Warren CareNet (https://www.care-net.org/roland-warren).

  "Don't you know that the runners in a stadium all race, but only one receives the prize? Run in such a way to win the prize. Now everyone who competes exercises self-control in everything. They do it to receive a perishable crown, but we an imperishable crown. So I do not run like one who runs aimlessly or box like one beating the air. Instead, *I discipline my body and bring it under strict control, so that after preaching to others, I myself will not be disqualified."* - 1 Corinthians 9:24-27 CSB

"Why be captivated, my son, by an immoral woman, or fondle the breasts of a promiscuous woman? For the LORD sees clearly what a man does, examining every path he takes. An evil man is held captive by his own sins; they are ropes that catch and hold him. *He will die for lack of self-control;* he will be lost because of his great foolishness." - Proverbs 5:20-23 NLT

- *Sexual immorality is part of the "earthly nature". You have a earthly nature and need to "kill it off".*

"Therefore, *put to death what belongs to your earthly nature*: sexual immorality, impurity, lust, evil desire, and greed, which is idolatry." - Colossians 3:5 CSB

- *When the temptation becomes fierce, focus on one day at a time.*

"Because of the LORD's faithful love we do not perish, for *his mercies never end.* They are new every morning; great is your faithfulness! I say, "The LORD is my portion, therefore I will put my hope in him."" - Lamentations 3:22-24 CSB

- *David and the affair with Bathsheba.* Obey the rules of sexual temptation - David breaks all of them. He acts the opposite of Joseph. Note that God considered sexual sin evil.

"Why then have you despised the LORD's command by *doing what I consider evil?* You struck down Uriah the Hethite with the sword and took his wife as your own wife -- you murdered him with the Ammonite's sword. Now therefore, the sword will never leave your house because you *despised me and took the wife of Uriah the Hethite to be your own wife.*" - 2 Samuel 12:9-10 CSB

Questions:

1. What does Romans 13:14 mean when it says "…don't make plans to gratify the desires of the flesh."?

2. What does the Apostle Paul mean in Colossians 3:5 when he says that sexual immorality (as well as the other listed sins) is "idolatry"?

3. What strategy did Moses use to avoid temptations in general?

4. How can sex be bad if it feels so good?

5. Does 1 Peter 3:3-4 mean I should not be concerned about my appearance?

Questions with suggested answers:

1. What does Romans 13:14 mean when it says "…don't make plans to gratify the desires of the flesh."?

Answer: Once you recognize the temptation that Satan is using (porn, movies, a specific person, or situation) to tempt you it is very important to not continue to think about it or put yourself into a situation where you could be sucked in. This strategy is important to use against any temptation but also works well with sexual temptation. For example, when I was in high school, I worked at a department store doing odd jobs. The CEO was a married man and many of the top management employees were women. This required many face to face meetings. I noted that his office wall was made of glass thus all the administrative assistants who sat outside his office were always able to see what was going on inside when he was meeting with women leaders. He also had a big desk that separated himself from the person being interviewed. Although I never spoke with him about this specific temptation, I suspect that this godly man (my Dad!) felt very aware of this temptation and was being proactive about it.

2. What does the Apostle Paul mean in Colossians 3:5 when he says that sexual immorality (as well as the other listed sins) is "idolatry"?

Answer: Sexual sins, along with the other sins listed are very physically (and sometimes emotionally) pleasurable in the moment to the person(s) committing the sin. Thus, these sins become addictive and very destructive and become an "idol" to the sinner. Remember, taking drugs, alcohol, eating a lot of chocolate, sky diving, driving fast etc.

can all be exhilarating for a moment and then the crash comes. Read Hebrews 11:24-26 above again regarding Moses' strategy. He did NOT deny that the activity was pleasurable but considered it short-lived and not worth risking his eternal destiny.

3. What strategy did Moses use to avoid temptations in general?

Answer: Moses used the strategy of "taking the long view". Moses grew up in Egypt and lived in luxury. He was exposed to all kinds of sin – money and privilege and polygamy. He never said that these were not fun or pleasurable. But he took the eternal view and wanted eternal rewards.

4. How can sex be bad if it feels so good?

Answer: The fact that it "feels good" is not a sign that it is right. Sex is designed to be pleasurable so as to bind a couple together in the marriage. A tightly bound couple can withstand many storms to a marriage. Many sensual activities outside marriage may be enticing but they bite you on the other side. Eating chocolate or other desserts are transient pleasure (and perfectly ok) but overdoing it leads to accumulation of calories that are tough to remove once turned into fat.

5. Does 1 Peter 3:3-4 mean I should not be concerned about my appearance?

Answer: "Don't let your beauty consist of outward things like elaborate hairstyles and wearing gold jewelry, but rather what is inside the heart -- the imperishable quality of a gentle and quiet spirit, which is of great worth in God's sight." - 1 Peter 3:3-4 CSB.

Peter is talking here about balance and perspective. There is nothing wrong with hair care, nail care etc. The point is sometimes we overemphasize our physical appearance and spend inordinate time (and money) on it. Peter is telling us to focus on our heart.

How should sexual sin in a Christ-follower be dealt with?

As discussed above, not all sexual sins are criminal or illegal. In other words, when two people willingly engage in sexual activity outside of marriage, in the United States the police will not show up and arrest them. However, if the activity falls into the category of sexual sin as defined by the Bible and the people involved claim to be Christians and are part of a local church then the Bible has something to say as to how we deal with that. Sadly, sexual sin does occur in the Church because it is composed of humans and wherever humans are there will be sexual temptations. Bill Newton discusses this in his book *Endure* on page 94 "After we come to faith in Christ, sin no longer reigns in us, *but it remains* (emphasis added)." In other words, even believers are vulnerable to sexual immorality. The Bible says that these sins in the Church must be dealt with and not tolerated, or they will actually spread similar to a little bread yeast affecting the whole loaf. Your boasting is not good. Don't you know that a little leaven leavens the whole batch of dough?" - 1 Corinthians 5:6 CSB.

There is an old saying, "public sin, public rebuke; private sin, private rebuke". When the sexual misconduct of Bill Hybels, then senior pastor of Willow Creek Church in Chicago, was exposed by an article in the Chicago Tribune newspaper in 2018 an investigation by the church was conducted. The results were released publicly, and he resigned. Public sin, public rebuke. This follows the guidance of the Scripture: "Publicly rebuke those who sin, so that the rest will be afraid." - 1 Timothy 5:20 CSB. However, sometimes a church member commits a moral sin (not criminal) that occurs privately. In the situation where the Christian repents (is sorry for the sin and turns from it) the case can be dealt with privately following the Biblical plans of church discipline discussed briefly below. This is not a "coverup" but since the situation has been resolved and a restoration plan instituted there is no reason for widespread public exposure and humiliation. Obviously, if the sin was criminal then this is in an entirely different situation which must be reported. If the person held a leadership position in the church, then additional steps would need to be taken.

• *We were not made for sexual sin. This is not the way God designed sex to be.*
1 Corinthians 6:12-17 CSB.

• *Sexual sins are different. It is a "sin against your own body". Your body is a temple of the Holy Spirit; do not misuse it.*
"Flee sexual immorality! Every other sin a person commits is outside the body, but the person who is sexually immoral sins against his own body. Don't you know that your body is a temple of the Holy Spirit who is in you, whom you have from God? You are not your own, for you were bought at a price. So glorify God with your body." - 1 Corinthians 6:18-20 CSB

• *Sexual immorality in church members is not to be tolerated,* especially if the offender(s) are not sorry for the sin or it is ongoing. Society may tolerate non-criminal sexual acts such as pornography and consensual sex outside marriage, but these are not to be tolerated in the Church. Recall that in the New Testament the term "sexual immorality" in the Greek is "porneia" from which we get the term pornography. It is a general term that covers all the sexual sins. It is less graphic than the Old Testament blunt descriptions of sexual sins.

"It is actually reported that there is sexual immorality among you, and the kind of sexual immorality that is not even tolerated among the Gentiles -- a man is sleeping with his father's wife. And you are arrogant! Shouldn't you be filled with grief and remove from your congregation the one who did this?" - 1 Corinthians 5:1-2 CSB

• *The church is to deal with issues in the church.* This is not referring to working or dealing with these people in the community. It is referring to a Christian who openly sins and keeps on sinning a sin of sexual immorality. It is also not referring to criminal sexual acts (rape, incest etc.).

"I wrote to you in a letter not to associate with sexually immoral people. I did not mean the immoral people of this world or the greedy and swindlers or idolaters; otherwise you would have to leave the world. But actually, I wrote you not to associate with anyone who claims to be a brother or sister and is sexually immoral or greedy, an idolater or verbally abusive, a drunkard or a swindler. Do not even eat with such a person. For what business is it of mine to judge outsiders? Don't you judge those who are inside? God judges outsiders. Remove the evil person from among you." - 1 Corinthians 5:9-13 CSB

• *Apostle's letter to the Gentile brothers and sisters in the Church.* The Greek word translated "sexual immorality" was again porneia. They were warned about sexual sins in the Church.

"They wrote: "From the apostles and the elders, your brothers, To the brothers and sisters among the Gentiles in Antioch, Syria, and Cilicia: Greetings. ..."For it was the Holy Spirit's decision -- and ours -- not to place further burdens on you beyond these requirements: "that you abstain from food offered to idols, from blood, from eating anything that has been strangled, and from sexual immorality. You will do well if you keep yourselves from these things. Farewell." - Acts 15:23, 28-29 CSB

• **Paul was concerned about sexual immorality (porneia) in the Church at Corinth.**
"I fear that when I come my God will again humiliate me in your presence, and I will grieve for many who sinned before and have not repented of the moral impurity, sexual immorality, and sensuality they practiced." - 2 Corinthians 12:21 CSB

• **Paul to Timothy regarding keeping order in the local church.** The word for sexually immoral here is pornos (male prostitute; one who does unlawful sexual intercourse). The word translated "homosexual" is arsenokoitēs which means someone who commits homosexual acts. These sins are part of the list of sins Paul discusses here. The other ones are more common.

1 Timothy 1:8-11 CSB

• **Paul to the local church at Thessalonica – control yourself!** Again, he warns in general against porneia (sexual immorality). We are to use the strategy of "keep away", "body control", "be holy". This verse also encourages us to have discipline in these areas.

"For this is God's will, your sanctification: that you keep away from sexual immorality, that each of you knows how to control his own body in holiness and honor, not with lustful passions, like the Gentiles, who don't know God. This means one must not transgress against and take advantage of a brother or sister in this manner, because the Lord is an avenger of all these offenses, as we also previously told and warned you. For God has not called us to impurity but to live in holiness. Consequently, anyone who rejects this does not reject man, but God, who gives you his Holy Spirit." - 1 Thessalonians 4:3-8 CSB

• **Paul says there is hope for those who have committed sin. It is possible to overcome these sins and tendencies and be forgiven and restored. Paul says some in the Church indeed had been that way but now were changed.**
The goal of dealing with sexual sin in the Church is to repent (be sorry and turn away from the sin), forgive and restore and Paul clearly states we can be cleansed of these sins. 1 Corinthians 6:9-11, Colossians 3:6-7

"And you were dead in your trespasses and sins in which you previously lived according to the ways of this world, according to the ruler of the power of the air, the spirit now working in the disobedient. We too all previously lived among them in our fleshly desires, carrying out the inclinations of our flesh and thoughts, and we were by nature children under wrath as the others were also." - Ephesians 2:1-3 CSB

Questions:

1. Why do popular people sometimes get caught in secret sins?

2. What happens to prominent people who sin in secret like this?

3. Why is the Church supposed to deal with non-criminal sexual sin?

Questions with suggested answers:

1. Why do popular people sometimes get caught in secret sins?

Answer: There is no shortage of articles or reports in the news these days of people getting charged with sexual sins. Sometimes these people are popular and well known and may even be pastors and religious workers. The charges are often hard to believe because the person on the outside may appear pious and righteous. Sexual sins are usually conducted in secrecy and sometimes the person who is the recipient of the sexual abuse is fearful to tell anyone. In fact, these sins may only be revealed years later. Remember, anyone is susceptible to these sins because they are human. Religious leaders and other famous people may be even more vulnerable because they feel this sin will not happen to them. They fail to be accountable to others and they put themselves into situations which make the temptation very strong. Remember, sex is tool number 1 in the Devil's Toolbox, and we all need to be aware of this to prevent falling into the Devil's trap. The temptation may be hottest for those doing God's work.

2. What happens to prominent people who sin in secret like this?

Answer: God does not tolerate sin for long. The truth usually comes out before or after the person dies. Some people take it to the grave without confessing. This happened with Ravi Zacharias. Ravi was a brilliant apologist who lectured around the world on matters of the Bible as well as authored many books. After he died of cancer it came to light that he had a secret life of sexual sin. This surprised many and took down his colleagues, family, and an entire organization. As Paul said to Timothy, "Some people's sins are obvious, preceding them to judgment, but the sins of others surface later." - 1 Timothy 5:24 CSB. It is to be remembered that God does not tolerate sin forever and sometimes He will simply terminate the person as He did with Er."Now Er, Judah's firstborn, was evil in the LORD's sight, *and the LORD put him to death*." - Genesis 38:7 CSB. Lastly, we must remember to not pre-judge the person because another form of evil is to falsely accuse someone of a sin or crime. Commandment 10 is "Do not give false testimony against your neighbor." - Exodus 20:16 CSB. Australian Catholic Cardinal George Pell who died January 10, 2023, was charged with sexual misconduct earlier in his life and imprisoned only to be fully exonerated by the High Court of Australia (Wall Street Journal January 12, 2023, article by Raymond de Souza).

3. Why is the Church supposed to deal with non-criminal sexual sin?

Answer: If the sin is criminal then obviously the legal system must be involved. However, let us use as an example a situation when a church member commits adultery. Adultery is not typically a criminal situation, but it is a violation of God's law (Commandment 7 "Do not commit adultery." - Exodus 20:14 CSB). God will not tolerate these sins. If the parties repent then restoration can occur; however, if the adultery continues without repentance, then the church will need to act and expel the guilty parties. Why? Because if unbelievers outside the church see open sin in church members they will say, "those Christians are no different than us – in fact, they are worse!". To keep the Church pure, we are to deal with church members (followers of Jesus) to move them to repentance and restoration. The goal is always restoration.

What if sexual sin occurs in the workplace?

These situations outside the Church, in the workplace for example, are different. Here, the place where you work will have a set of rules regarding sexual harassment. Paul makes it clear that he is not asking us to be total separatists and indeed most places where we work, we interact with colleagues and customers who are non-believers and may follow a completely different moral code. The verses below discuss what the Bible says about sexual sin *outside the Church*.

• *We will work and interact with people who may be sexually immoral or have very different views on this topic than we do. It is different with believers vs non-believers.*
1 Corinthians 5:9-11

• *We are always to try and avoid these situations outside or inside the Church.*
1 Corinthians 6:18-20

• *We are not to sexually harass people anywhere and it is not allowed in the workplace.* This is mentioned in the book of Ruth and was considered bad and humiliating. This is a very important verse to understand – sexual harassment in the workplace is not to be tolerated.

"See which field they are harvesting and follow them. *Haven't I ordered the young men not to touch you?* When you are thirsty, go and drink from the jars the young men have filled." ... When she got up to gather grain, Boaz ordered his young men, "Let her even gather grain among the bundles, and *don't humiliate her.*" - Ruth 2:9, 15 CSB

• *Paul says to not tell or participate in sexual jokes.* This can occur in some workplaces. Why? Because they will stimulate lustful thoughts and interest in sex that is not good for the mind. This is the real problem with watching movies and reading books that are highly sexual.

"But sexual immorality and any impurity or greed should not even be heard of among you, as is proper for saints. *Obscene and foolish talking or crude joking are not suitable, but rather giving thanks.* For know and recognize this: Every sexually immoral or impure or greedy person, who is an idolater, does not have an inheritance in the kingdom of Christ and of God." - Ephesians 5:3-5 CSB

"But now, put away all the following: anger, wrath, malice, slander, and *filthy language* from your mouth." - Colossians 3:8 CSB

• *Be disciplined. You are not without control; not helpless.* We are under no obligation to live like this. At some point it takes plain old discipline in addition to the help from the Holy Spirit.

"For a man's ways are before the LORD's eyes, and he considers all his paths. A wicked man's iniquities will trap him; he will become tangled in the ropes of his own sin. *He will die because there is no discipline, and be lost because of his great stupidity.*" - Proverbs 5:21-23 CSB

"Therefore do not let sin reign in your mortal body, so that you obey its desires. And do not offer any parts of it to sin as weapons for unrighteousness. But as those who are alive from the dead, *offer yourselves to God, and all the parts of yourselves to God as weapons for righteousness. For sin will not rule over you, because you are not under the law but under grace.*" - Romans 6:12-14 CSB

• Discipline + the Holy Spirit.
"So then, brothers and sisters, *we are not obligated to the flesh to live according to the flesh, because if you live according to the flesh, you are going to die.* But if by the Spirit you put to death the deeds of the body, you will live." - Romans 8:12-13 CSB

• Don't make it easy to sin in the workplace.
"But put on the Lord Jesus Christ, and *don't make plans to gratify the desires of the flesh.*"
- Romans 13:14 CSB

Summary: Since the workplace is not your church the rules may be somewhat different as to how these issues are handled. In 2023, it has become very evident that sexual harassment is not to be tolerated in the workplace. Many leaders and executives, mostly men along with some women, have lost their job because of violation of workplace rules. In 2021 the former governor of New York, Andrew Cuomo resigned because of sexual harassment in the workplace. In 2022, the CEO of CNN Jeff Zucker resigned/fired because of a consensual relationship with Allison Gollust. She was an executive vice president under his command for many years. She too lost her job. This was not harassment; rather it was considered wrong because of the potential to interfere with business and fairness to other employees. It broke the rules of CNN. Thus, the rules put in place in the Bible are also very relevant today for the workplace.

Question with suggested answer:

1. We know that people of the opposite sex will work together in teams at work or in school or even church. How do we conduct these important and necessary business relationships and get work done without falling into sexual sin?

Answer: Remember, we are there to work not to socialize, although social events can certainly be a part of team building. Work meetings are necessary but should be as open as possible and in teams. Understand your boundaries as discussed above. Can you have lunch in the open cafeteria with another of the opposite sex? Can you share a taxi to the airport? Can you rent a car and take a long trip with another of the opposite sex or the sex you are attracted to? Can you have a 1:1 meeting in the lobby of the meeting hotel? What if the boss invites you to have that 1:1 business discussion in their hotel suite? Can you compliment a person on their new hair design, glasses, dress or suit or tie? A good solution is to follow Romans 13:14 "But put on the Lord Jesus Christ, and *don't make plans to gratify the desires of the flesh.*" That means don't let yourself be put into a situation that might lend itself to trouble. In general, having meetings in the open, with the door open or always taking an additional person along increase the chances of safety. The more private the meeting and once sexual arousal occurs the ability of your conscience to avoid the temptation is markedly reduced.

5

Does God Allow Freedom of Choice?

Serving Christ and following the teachings of the Bible is not burdensome but rather frees us from the consequences of sin. Sometimes people say that Christianity is restrictive and that they want to "be free to run their own life". God gives us clear instructions regarding the rules and what He expects of us, but also gives us freedom of choice to make decisions. Even the decision to become a Christ-follower is never forced upon the person. However, whatever we choose – to follow Jesus or not – we bear the consequences and they are eternal. Below are several Biblical examples where people were given a choice.

Adam and Eve in the Garden of Eden.

• God gave Adam and Eve a commandment, but it came with boundaries and responsibilities. They chose to go their own way instead of God's way. They thought they knew better; instead, they believed a lie and it caused death.
"And the LORD God commanded the man, "You are free to eat from any tree of the garden, "but you must not eat from the tree of the knowledge of good and evil, for on the day you eat from it, you will certainly die." - Genesis 2:16-17 CSB

Abram and Sarai and the promise of an heir.

• God promised to give Abram and Sarai children in Genesis 13
"After Lot had separated from him, the LORD said to Abram, "Look from the place where you are. Look north and south, east and west, "for I will give you and your offspring forever all the land that you see."I will make your offspring like the dust of the earth, so that if anyone could count the dust of the earth, then your offspring could be counted." - Genesis 13:14-16 CSB

• *By Genesis 15 Abram begins to doubt that this will happen since he and Sarai remain childless. It appeared his inheritance would go to their servant Eliezer.*
Genesis 15:1-6

• *Although Abram and Sarai had clearly heard the promise of God, when the children did not come, they became impatient and took the situation into their own hands.* They chose to have a child with the household slave girl Hagar. This cultural adultery led to jealousy, abuse, and child abandonment. God will let us sin if we purpose to do so – He will not force you to obey – but we bear the consequences and so do others downstream of the sin.

"Abram's wife Sarai had not borne any children for him, but she owned an Egyptian slave named Hagar. Sarai said to Abram, "Since the LORD has prevented me from bearing children, go to my slave; perhaps through her I can build a family." And Abram agreed to what Sarai said. So Abram's wife Sarai took Hagar, her Egyptian slave, and gave her to her husband Abram as a wife for him. This happened after Abram had lived in the land of Canaan ten years. He slept with Hagar, and she became pregnant. When she saw that she was pregnant, her mistress became contemptible to her." - Genesis 16:1-4 CSB

Satan as an angel in Heaven and had been given a choice.

• *He chose to rebel against God; was rejected and left to deceive people on earth.*
"Shining morning star, how you have fallen from the heavens! You destroyer of nations, you have been cut down to the ground. You said to yourself, "I will ascend to the heavens; I will set up my throne above the stars of God. I will sit on the mount of the gods' assembly, in the remotest parts of the North."I will ascend above the highest clouds; I will make myself like the Most High." But you will be brought down to Sheol into the deepest regions of the Pit. Those who see you will stare at you; they will look closely at you: "Is this the man who caused the earth to tremble, who shook the kingdoms, "who turned the world into a wilderness, who destroyed its cities and would not release the prisoners to return home? " - Isaiah 14:12-17 CSB

• *Jesus was present when Satan disobeyed and was ejected from Heaven.*
"He said to them, "I watched Satan fall from heaven like lightning." - Luke 10:18 CSB

• *Satan now torments people on earth to do evil and make wrong choices.*
Genesis 3:1-7

• *Satan is out to kill and destroy.*
"A thief comes only to steal and kill and destroy. I have come so that they may have life and have it in abundance." - John 10:10 CSB

• *Because of Satan, evil and sin in the world, you will be faced with choices every day. This will interfere with your desire to do good. It will be a choice.*
"The sinful nature wants to do evil, which is just the opposite of what the Spirit wants. And the Spirit gives us desires that are the opposite of what the sinful nature desires. These two forces are constantly fighting each other, so you are not free to carry out your good intentions." - Galatians 5:17 NLT

Other angels were also given a choice; some disobeyed and joined Satan.

"And I remind you of the *angels who did not stay within the limits of authority* God gave them but left the place where they belonged. God has kept them chained in prisons of darkness, waiting for the day of judgment." Jude 1:6, NLT.

God has a choice too …sometimes He chooses for unclear reasons.

• *He chose the nation of Israel to bring the Messiah Jesus into the world.*
"But the LORD selected you and brought you out of Egypt's iron furnace to be a people for his inheritance, as you are today." - Deuteronomy 4:20 CSB

Deuteronomy 10:15 CSB

"For the LORD has chosen Jacob for himself, Israel for his own special treasure." Psalms 135:4, NLT.
Romans 8:29, 30, NLT.

• *God chose Ephraim over Manasseh despite his being younger; it was God's choice.*
Genesis 48:8-20 CSB

• *God chose Joshua to lead the Israelites into the Promised Land despite the pleas of Moses.*
"Please let me cross over and see the beautiful land on the other side of the Jordan, that good hill country and Lebanon. But the LORD was angry with me because of you and

would not listen to me. The LORD said to me, That's enough! Do not speak to me again about this matter. Go to the top of Pisgah and look to the west, north, south, and east, and see it with your own eyes, for you will not cross the Jordan. But commission Joshua and encourage and strengthen him, for he will cross over ahead of the people and enable them to inherit this land that you will see." - Deuteronomy 3:25-28 CSB

Moses gave the Israelites a choice as to whether to follow God. He clearly laid out the consequences of the choice – life or death, prosperity, or disaster.
Deuteronomy 30:15-20

Joshua gave the people a choice.

"But if you are unwilling to serve the LORD, *then choose today whom you will serve.* Would you prefer the gods your ancestors served beyond the Euphrates? Or will it be the gods of the Amorites in whose land you now live? *But as for me and my family, we will serve the LORD.*" Joshua 24:15, NLT.

Deborah gave Barak a choice with its consequences.
Judges 4:9, 10

David chose to go God's way and follow His principles as outlined in the Bible. Choosing to follow God's path demonstrates our faith in Him.

"I hate those who are undecided about you, *but my choice is clear--I love your law.*" Psalms 119:113, NLT.
Psalms 119:30

Jesus never forced people to believe in Him. Following Jesus is a choice.

• *Jesus is never forced onto people – He knocks... the latch is on the inside.*
"Look! I stand at the door and knock. If you hear my voice and open the door, I will come in, and we will share a meal together as friends." - Revelation 3:20 NLT

• *He told the disciples to give them the message and if they reject it to move on. The people that reject will bear the consequences of their choice.*
"If the people of the village won't receive your message when you enter it, shake off its dust from your feet as you leave. It is a sign that you have abandoned that village to its fate." Luke 9:5, NLT.

God gave you a conscience and you need to obey it.

• *The type of food you eat is a personal choice – you are free to eat whatever.*
"I know and am perfectly sure on the authority of the Lord Jesus that no food, in and of itself, is wrong to eat. *But if someone believes it is wrong, then for that person it is wrong.*" Romans 14:14, NLT.

• *Paul lived his life in synchrony with his conscience.*
"Paul looked straight at the Sanhedrin and said, "Brothers, I have lived my life before God in all good conscience to this day." - Acts 23:1 CSB

Peter and the apostles when faced with a choice, obeyed God above the civil authorities.

"The captain went with his Temple guards and arrested the apostles, but without violence, for they were afraid the people would stone them. Then they brought the apostles before the high council, where the high priest confronted them. Didn't we tell you never again to teach in this man's name? he demanded. Instead, you have filled all Jerusalem with your teaching about him, and you want to make us responsible for his death! But Peter and the apostles replied, *We must obey God rather than any human authority.*" - Acts 5:26-29 NLT

Missionary service involves a choice – the case of Titus.

"Thanks be to God, who put the same concern for you into the heart of Titus.

For he welcomed our appeal and, being very diligent, *went out to you by his own choice.*" 2 Corinthians 8:16, 17, CSB.

Questions:

1. Why did God allow us to make our own choice?

2. God chose Israel (see Deut 10:15). If He did that then how can we explain the later verses saying God is impartial. "For the LORD your God is the God of gods and Lord of lords, the great, mighty, and awe-inspiring God, showing no partiality and taking no bribe. He executes justice for the fatherless and the widow, and loves the resident alien, giving him food and clothing." - Deuteronomy 10:17-18 CSB

3. In 2024, if you say, "I am pro-choice", what do most people think you are talking about?

4. Can you think of an example in modern history where people had to obey God rather than the civil authorities? What were the consequences?

Questions with suggested answers:

1. Why did God allow us to make our own choice?

Answer: God wanted us to be obedient and love Him and follow Him willingly. True love is not forced. These verses are critical to understanding how God gives us free will. Before the time of the Earth, we see that angels were given a choice – Lucifer (an angel, also known as Satan or the Devil) rebelled and took other angels (today's demons) with him. Satan is then in the Garden at the time of Earth's creation. Adam and Eve were given an immediate choice – and both failed and sin entered the world. Abram and Sarai were allowed to "choose to sin" and thus the firstborn to Abram was Ishmael whose descendants are the Arabic people of today. Similarly, today we are never forced to follow God or His ways. God gives each of us choice. We live in a world that has suffered greatly from the choices of Adam and Eve. Now, the choice is ours – will we follow God's way? It has great consequences not only to us but the people around us.

2. God chose Israel (see Deut 10:15). If He did that then how can we explain the later verses saying God is impartial. "For the LORD your God is the God of gods and Lord of lords, the great, mighty, and awe-inspiring God, showing no partiality and taking no bribe. He executes justice for the fatherless and the widow, and loves the resident alien, giving him food and clothing." - Deuteronomy 10:17-18 CSB

Answer: The choice of the Israelites was to bring Jesus, the Messiah into the world. It is clear from the Gospels (and the verses from Deuteronomy 10:17-18) that God cares about all people groups and salvation is open to all.

3. In 2024, if you say, "I am pro-choice", what do most people think you are talking about?

Answer: This term is usually used in reference to what you believe about the right to a non-medical abortion (an abortion done for no medical reason in the mother or child). It refers to a woman's choice to have that abortion. There are 4 people involved in any non-medical abortion – the man who got the woman pregnant, the woman who participated in the consensual act (we are talking about non-criminal situations), the child, and the physician or other health care professional that prescribes the pills or does the procedure. Since the baby cannot speak for themself, society currently gives the decision of the child to the mother. Since we have right of conscience laws, no person involved in health care (physician, pharmacist, nurse etc.,) can be forced to perform a non-medical abortion if it is against his or her conscience. So, although the Bible would support the fact that a child *in utero* is a person recognized by God and thus entitled to life, God permits the woman to proceed with an abortion. As outlined above – your choices have consequences. Adam and Eve chose to disobey, and the consequences were brutal to all of us. The choice to kill an unborn child frees the mother and father of responsibility of caring for the child but the consequences will only be fully understood in eternity. These kinds of choices are weighty and have huge implications. Our goal should be to get men and women to understand the full consequences of the first act – the intercourse that led to the pregnancy. If they would consider that initial choice, it would never come to a choice of abortion.

4. Can you think of an example in modern history where people had to obey God rather than the civil authorities? What were the consequences?

Answer: In the United States we have protections in place so that we are not forced to do something against our religion or conscience. These can be found at https://www.hhs.gov/conscience/conscience-protections/index.html. Many people around the world live under oppressive regimes that do not tolerate dissent. This can result in loss of life. We refer to this as becoming a martyr. An example is Dietrich Bonhoeffer, a German Lutheran pastor and theologian who was a founder of the Confessing Church that resisted the Nazis during WWII. His resistance and outspoken speeches against Hitler led to his arrest and execution in the Flossenburg Concentration Camp on April 9, 1945. He was martyred for his faith.

Thomas Witzig

6

Career Planning
What Should I Do with the
Next Phase of My Life?

No matter where you are at in your life's journey there will always be a next step. If you are young, this will be planning for a vocation. If nearing retirement age it will be planning on how to invest in this phase of life so as to continue in your service to God. God is interested in helping with these decisions. The verses in Chapters 1 and 2 are also very relevant for planning in that understanding "who am I" and "how to determine the will of God" are foundational to understand what God wants for you in this next phase. It may be useful to review those verses before reading this chapter.

Plan well. Follow God's advice as outlined in the Bible. Following Jesus is the most important first step. It will spare you from falling into the devil's traps and diverting from God's plan for you.

"My child, don't lose sight of good planning and insight. Hang on to them, for the LORD is your security. He will keep your foot from being caught in a trap." Proverbs 3:21, 26, NLT.

• *God has a specific plan for you.*
Psalm 139:13-18

• *God knows the whole plan right now; we don't! Be patient.*
"Listen to me, descendants of Jacob, all you who remain in Israel. I have cared for you since you were born. *Yes, I carried you before you were born. I will be your God throughout your lifetime--until your hair is white with age.* I made you, and I will care for you. I will carry you along and save you." - Isaiah 46:3-4 NLT

• *God wants the best for you. Listen to Him through the words of Scripture – don't be stubborn.*

"The LORD says, "I will guide you along the best pathway for your life. I will advise you and watch over you. Do not be like a senseless horse or mule that needs a bit and bridle to keep it under control." Many sorrows come to the wicked, but unfailing love surrounds those who trust the LORD. So rejoice in the LORD and be glad, all you who obey him! Shout for joy, all you whose hearts are pure!" - Psalm 32:8-11 NLT

• *God made you special. He cares for you. The plans for you will be worked out as you travel the road of life.*

"*The LORD will work out his plans for my life*--for your faithful love, O LORD, endures forever. Don't abandon me, for you made me." Psalms 138:8, NLT.

• *Ultimately you are part of the plan to bring people to Jesus.*

"When he saw the crowds, he felt compassion for them, because they were distressed and dejected, like sheep without a shepherd. Then he said to his disciples, the harvest is abundant, but the workers are few. Therefore, pray to the Lord of the harvest to send out workers into his harvest." - Matthew 9:36-38 CSB

• *Honor and glorify God in whatever the next step is.*

"*Commit your activities to the LORD*, and your plans will be established." - Proverbs 16:3 CSB

"So, whether you eat or drink, or whatever you do, *do everything for the glory of God*." - 1 Corinthians 10:31 CSB

John 4:34

The work you do for the Lord is never wasted.

• *Be excited about your vocation.*

"So, my dear brothers and sisters, be strong and immovable. Always work enthusiastically for the Lord, for you know that nothing you do for the Lord is ever useless." - 1 Corinthians 15:58 NLT

• *Have a healthy and realistic view of what God wants for you.*

"Because of the privilege and authority God has given me, I give each of you this warning: *Don't think you are better than you really are. Be honest in your evaluation of yourselves, measuring yourselves by the faith God has given us.* " - Romans 12:3 NLT

Focus on taking the next step.

• The directions may be very clear as they were to Abram (Abraham).
"Then the LORD told Abram, "Leave your country, your relatives, and your father's house, and go to the land that I will show you. I will cause you to become the father of a great nation. I will bless you and make you famous, and I will make you a blessing to others. I will bless those who bless you and curse those who curse you. All the families of the earth will be blessed through you." Genesis 12:1-3, NLT.

• God usually reveals only enough direction for the next step. In the case of Saul, it was simply, "Go to Damascus".
"As I was on the road, approaching Damascus about noon, a very bright light from heaven suddenly shone down around me. I fell to the ground and heard a voice saying to me, 'Saul, Saul, why are you persecuting me?' 'Who are you, lord?' I asked. And the voice replied, 'I am Jesus the Nazarene, the one you are persecuting.' The people with me saw the light but didn't understand the voice speaking to me. *I asked, 'What should I do, Lord?' And the Lord told me, 'Get up and go into Damascus, and there you will be told everything you are to do.'*" - Acts 22:6-10 NLT

• Don't tackle the whole plan all at once – break it down into manageable parts. Note what God said to the Israelites about conquering the land.
"The LORD your God will drive out these nations before you little by little. You will not be able to destroy them all at once; otherwise, the wild animals will become too numerous for you." - Deuteronomy 7:22 CSB

• Keep your eye on the ultimate goal. Do not get sidetracked.
"Look straight ahead, and fix your eyes on what lies before you. Mark out a straight path for your feet; stay on the safe path. Don't get sidetracked; keep your feet from following evil." – Proverbs 4:25-27 NLT

Remember Jesus leads and we "follow"; do not get out ahead of Him.

• When you become a follower of Jesus you dedicate your life and plans to Him and "you follow".
Romans 12:1

"*If anyone serves me, he must follow me.* Where I am, there my servant also will be. If anyone serves me, the Father will honor him." - John 12:26 CSB

• *Let God direct you.*

"Don't copy the behavior and customs of this world, *but let God transform you* into a new person by changing the way you think. Then you will learn to know God's will for you, which is good and pleasing and perfect." - Romans 12:2 NLT

What are your spiritual gifts? You will have some but not all of these.

• *Your gifts are to be used for the betterment and service to the entire body of Christ. We are all in this life together.*

"Now as we have many parts in one body, and all the parts do not have the same function, in the same way we who are many are one body in Christ and individually members of one another. According to the grace given to us, we have different gifts: If prophecy, use it according to the proportion of one's faith; if service, use it in service; if teaching, in teaching; if exhorting, in exhortation; giving, with generosity; leading, with diligence; showing mercy, with cheerfulness." - Romans 12:4-8 CSB

• *Don't compare yourself to others; nobody gets everything, but we all get one or some spiritual gifts. Evaluate your gifts and use them for the glory of God.*

"And he himself gave some to be apostles, some prophets, some evangelists, some pastors and teachers, equipping the saints for the work of ministry, to build up the body of Christ, until we all reach unity in the faith and in the knowledge of God's Son, growing into maturity with a stature measured by Christ's fullness." - Ephesians 4:11-13 CSB

• *Make certain that you love people in your vocation.*

"Don't just pretend to love others. *Really love them.* Hate what is wrong. Hold tightly to what is good. Love each other with genuine affection, and take delight in honoring each other." - Romans 12:9-10 NLT

• *Work hard; be enthusiastic.*

"Never be lazy, but *work hard and serve the Lord enthusiastically.* Rejoice in our confident hope. Be patient in trouble, and keep on praying. When God's people are in need, be ready to help them. Always be eager to practice hospitality." - Romans 12:11-13 NLT

"Let each person examine his own work, and then he can take pride in himself alone, and not compare himself with someone else. For each person will have to carry his own load." - Galatians 6:4-5 CSB

• **Be happy to follow the Lord's instructions.**

"How happy is the one who does not walk in the advice of the wicked or stand in the pathway with sinners or sit in the company of mockers! Instead, his delight is in the LORD's instruction, and he meditates on it day and night. He is like a tree planted beside flowing streams that bears its fruit in its season and whose leaf does not wither. Whatever he does prospers." - Psalm 1:1-3 CSB

Summary: When it comes to career planning it is important to evaluate yourself in light of how God made you. What are your interests? What are you really good at? What era are you living in? Pastor Rick Warren in his book *The Purpose Driven Life* wrote this regarding career planning - "You will be most effective when you use your spiritual gifts and abilities in the area of your heart's desire and in a way that best expresses your personality and experiences. The better the fit, the more successful you will be." If you have a passion for science and caring for the sick, then medicine is a great field for you. If you can hit home runs like Aaron Judge of the New York Yankees, then pursue baseball and God will be pleased and bless your work. Your plans will also be dictated by events beyond your control. What if you lived in Ukraine in 2022-2024? Your plans to go to college or work in a certain area have likely been totally disrupted by the war. Your college career may have been derailed or completely changed by COVID-19. Hurricane Ian may have wiped out your Ft Myers home in September 2022 and you had to move. Your home and family destroyed in minutes by the destructive earthquake in Turkey and Syria in February 2023 or the Lahaina wildfire of August 2023. Often these types of unpredictable events will force you to change your plan. Sometimes the results when viewed many years later will seem to have resulted in "some good coming out of a bad situation". In other circumstances you will never ever understand until eternity why the event happened and cannot see any good that ever came out of it.

Questions:

1. How does being a follower of Jesus affect your choice of vocation?

2. What types of jobs does God want me to do?

3. How do you get good advice from others?

4. Why is it important to get career planning right early in life (like before 25)?

5. What's in your dash?

6. Psalm 138:8 says "The LORD will work out his plans for my life…" What does that mean to you?

7. How do I pick a college or technical school to go to?

Questions with suggested answers:

1. How does being a follower of Jesus affect your choice of vocation?

Answer: It means that you will pray for God's guidance as you evaluate your career plans. As a Christian, you will also not choose a vocation that involves sin. For example, if you were an actor you would need to select roles that would not compromise your witness. As a medical doctor, you would need to join a group that would respect your views on life. You would not want to be forced into having to euthanize a patient or do abortions for no medical reason.

2. What types of jobs does God want me to do?

Answer: God gives us many gifts and talents. We know from the Bible that He endowed some to be designers of the Tabernacle because they had special artistic skills.

"Moses then said to the Israelites: Look, the LORD has appointed by name Bezalel son of Uri, son of Hur, of the tribe of Judah. He has filled him with God's Spirit, with wisdom, understanding, and ability in every kind of craft "to design artistic works in gold, silver, and bronze, "to cut gemstones for mounting, and to carve wood for work in every kind of artistic craft. He has also given both him and Oholiab son of Ahisamach, of the tribe of Dan, the ability to teach others. He has filled them with skill to do all the work of a gem cutter; a designer; an embroiderer in blue, purple, and scarlet yarn and fine linen; and a weaver. They can do every kind of craft and design artistic designs." - Exodus 35:30-35 CSB. Then there was Nimrod, who was a skilled hunter. Cush fathered Nimrod, who began to be powerful in the land. He was a powerful hunter in the sight of the LORD. That is why it is said, "Like Nimrod, a powerful hunter in the sight of the LORD." - Genesis 10:8-9 CSB. Luke was a physician and writer of the Book of Luke.

"Luke, the dearly loved physician, and Demas send you greetings." - Colossians 4:14 CSB. What are you really good at? What excites you? Did your teacher/professor ever say to you, "you are really gifted in the area of X, you should pursue that". Some of these desires and talents were gifted to us in our DNA and the way were designed by God.

3. How do you get good advice from others?

Answer: You have to be careful here. Some career advisors may not be honest with you – they may be too positive or too negative. Some will try to discourage you on purpose so as to "see what you are made of". This will especially happen if you are trying out for a Special Forces position in the military such as a Navy Seal, Air Force Combat Rescue Officer, or a Coast Guard rescue swimmer. Your application for graduate or medical school may be rejected and you will need to decide how to handle this. This is where you need to get several advisors and then look deep within yourself for the drive, persistence, and resilience to achieve your goal. Seek out advice from your parents and also mature men and women in your church that can speak from experiences they have had in their careers. You will also benefit from a good mentor. Joshua was mentored by Moses: "The LORD would speak with Moses face to face, just as a man speaks with his friend, then Moses would return to the camp. His assistant, the young man Joshua son of Nun, would not leave the inside of the tent." - Exodus 33:11 CSB

4. Why is it important to get career planning right early in life (like before 25)?

Answer: Although you can often make a career change later in life it is important to not make major mistakes in the first 4-8 years after high school as these can make it difficult to get back on track. What are some examples of these errors? I recall several of my classmates who goofed off in their first year of college and received bad grades; then later wanted to go to medical school. Some of them were never able to recover from this poor showing. Cheating in school or on the job can stain your reputation. Having a child out of wedlock will require long-term childcare and support. Committing a crime will make certain vocations impossible. Addictions (drugs and alcohol) can cripple your life. Early marriage itself is not a barrier because often 2 can live cheaper than one. Early children in that marriage could temporarily delay a career but it's the single parent situation that makes it financially and emotionally difficult for both the single parent and the child . Getting a college or technical degree is important because it lays the foundation for many vocations. It's so easy to do that starting at age 18 and getting it done by 22. It is key to focus hard on general career planning in these early years.

5. What's in your dash?

Answer: When you visit a cemetery or monument to a person, the date of birth and death of the occupant is engraved on the stone. Right now, mine reads January 1, 1953 - ___.

The date of my death has not yet been determined as of the time of this book. So, the time between our "dash" is "our time; our age; our chance to make a difference". God placed us here for a reason – go for it; enjoy it; and look forward to eternity. Have a "great run"!

6. Psalm 138:8 says "The LORD will work out his plans for my life…" What does that mean to you?

Answer: The concept here is that God is constantly working in your life. There will be all kinds of things that may happen to you that will seemingly derail your plans. If you feel comfortable share these with your friends or study group. In the midst of all of these God is still working. Watch how He uses events to shape you and your career.

7. How do I pick a college or technical school to go to?

Answer: Pick a place with great teachers that will teach the truth and how to think critically. The educational experience should allow you to freely ask great questions and grow. "For the time will come when people will not tolerate sound doctrine, but according to their own desires, will multiply teachers for themselves because they have an itch to hear what they want to hear." - 2 Timothy 4:3 CSB. "I solemnly charge you before God and Christ Jesus, who is going to judge the living and the dead, and because of his appearing and his kingdom: Preach the word; be ready in season and out of season; rebuke, correct, and encourage with great patience and teaching." - 2 Timothy 4:1-2 CSB

7

How to Have a Quiet Time in a Very Loud World

As we live our lives as a follower of Jesus it is important to be in close communication with Him. God wants to have a relationship with us. For example, God told Abram in Genesis 17:1 "When Abram was ninety-nine years old, the LORD appeared to him, saying, "I am God Almighty. *Live in my presence and be blameless*." To live in God's presence means that we receive guidance by reading and meditating on the Bible. To do that we need to carve out some time from our busy schedules to let God speak to us. We hear His voice not audibly, but through Scripture and the influence of the Holy Spirit. A "quiet time" is sometimes called "meditation time". We can meditate as we walk through nature, read at the kitchen table, or listen to Scripture as we take our daily commute. It should be a time of our choosing and does not need to be long – perhaps 15 minutes. Some like to read a devotional book but make sure it is packed with Scripture and not just stories. When reading, ask, "What is this passage saying to me today?" Often, we will be reading a passage that we have read many times before but *today* it will speak to us in a way that is particularly relevant to our current situation. That is the work of the Holy Spirit. In the end it is not difficult to get Scripture into our lives, but we do have to make the effort – *meditation and prayer are spiritual disciplines*.

• *Whom should we meditate on? Jesus! David says, "I meditate on YOU God!"*
"When I think of you as I lie on my bed, I meditate on you during the night watches because you are my helper; I will rejoice in the shadow of your wings. I follow close to you; your right hand holds on to me." - Psalm 63:6-8 CSB

• *What to meditate on? David meditated on the ways of God.*
"*I will meditate on your precepts* and think about your ways. I will delight in your statutes; I will not forget your word." - Psalm 119:15-16 CSB

• *When should we meditate? Isaac meditated during an evening walk. Some people like to pray and listen to God's Word when walking or hiking.*

"Meanwhile, Isaac, whose home was in the Negev, had returned from Beer-lahai-roi. *One evening as he was walking and meditating in the fields,* he looked up and saw the camels coming." - Genesis 24:62-63 NLT

• *What does meditation accomplish? It "stills and quiets" like a baby quieted by its mother.*

"LORD, my heart is not proud; my eyes are not haughty. I do not get involved with things too great or too wondrous for me. *Instead, I have calmed and quieted my soul like a weaned child with its mother; my soul is like a weaned child.*" - Psalm 131:1-2 CSB

• *How often should we meditate? BID—the medical abbreviation for "twice a day".*

"How happy is the one who does not walk in the advice of the wicked or stand in the pathway with sinners or sit in the company of mockers! Instead, his delight is in the LORD's instruction, *and he meditates on it day and night.*" - Psalm 1:1-2 CSB

• *What parts of our body are involved? We meditate in our heart and mind.*

"May the words of my mouth and the meditation of my heart be acceptable to you, LORD, my rock and my Redeemer." - Psalm 19:14 CSB

• *Meditating is thinking or dwelling on things that are true; honorable; pure; lovely; virtuous; and worthy of praise. Note the quality of the things to meditate on.*

"Finally brothers and sisters, whatever is true, whatever is honorable, whatever is just, whatever is pure, whatever is lovely, whatever is commendable -- if there is any moral excellence and if there is anything praiseworthy -- *dwell on these things.*" - Philippians 4:8 CSB The KJV version of this same verse is beautiful - "Finally, brethren, whatever things are true, whatever things are noble, whatever things are just, whatever things are pure, whatever things are lovely, whatever things are of good report, if there is any virtue and if there is anything praiseworthy--meditate on these things." - Philippians 4:8 NKJV

Question with suggested answer:

1. Why is it important to specifically meditate on the things mentioned in Phil 4:8? How does this relate to the constant newsfeeds we take in through social media, the internet, and the movies we watch?

Answer: This verse tells us what to watch, listen to, or read. You have control over the input into your brain. How do you feel after you watch a movie that went too far in the sexual scenes? Can you listen to provocative music? What about horror movies showing demons and the occult? You may think you can handle it but what you will learn is that the devil will "replay" these visuals over and over in your mind. God tells us instead to focus and input information about true, pure, noble, and lovely things. Put a strong set of controls on what enters your brain through your eyes and ears.

What does meditation accomplish? Our view of meditation is often influenced by what we see people doing during yoga or other mystical acts. *God provides an entirely different view of meditation in these verses.* When we meditate, we focus on God and the Scriptures not on ourselves or problems. Our meditation time should be a time of reflection on God, not a mindless focus on nothingness.

• *Meditation if done properly pleases and honors God.*
"I will sing to the LORD all my life; I will sing praise to my God while I live. *May my meditation be pleasing to him;* I will rejoice in the LORD." - Psalm 104:33-34 CSB

• *Proper meditation keeps the focus on the LORD.*
"*I always let the LORD guide me.* Because he is at my right hand, I will not be shaken. Therefore my heart is glad and my whole being rejoices; my body also rests securely." - Psalm 16:8-9 CSB

• *Meditation should remind us that God loves us and wants to be with us.*
"For God loved the world in this way: He gave his one and only Son, so that everyone who believes in him will not perish but have eternal life." - John 3:16 CSB
Genesis 17:1

• *Meditation time is thinking time. David found it delightful.*
"I will meditate on your precepts and think about your ways. I will delight in your statutes; *I will not forget your word.*" - Psalm 119:15-16 CSB

• *Meditation places Scripture into our lives; like recharging a battery.*
"How can a young man keep his way pure? *By keeping your word.* I have sought you with all my heart; don't let me wander from your commands. I have treasured your word in my heart so that I may not sin against you." - Psalm 119:9-11 CSB

• *Meditation is a time of instruction as God reveals truth into our lives.*
"This book of instruction must not depart from your mouth; *you are to meditate on it day and night so that you may carefully observe everything written in it.* For then you will prosper and succeed in whatever you do." - Joshua 1:8 CSB

• *God counsels us during our meditation time. God even works in your sleep by renewing your mind! It helps us discern the will of God.*
"I will bless the LORD who counsels me -- *even at night when my thoughts trouble me.*" - Psalm 16:7 CSB

"Do not be conformed to this age, but *be transformed by the renewing of your mind*, so that you may discern what is the good, pleasing, and perfect will of God." - Romans 12:2 CSB

• *Meditation is reflection; reflection does not come quickly; rather, it requires time like a cow chews its cud—reflecting and digesting the truth.*
"I remember the days of old; I meditate on all you have done; I reflect on the work of your hands." - Psalm 143:5 CSB

• *Confession can be spurred during a time of meditation.*
"If we confess our sins, he is faithful and righteous to forgive us our sins and to cleanse us from all unrighteousness." - 1 John 1:9 CSB

What does prayer and meditation involve?

•*Appreciating the splendor of God in nature. Beautiful scenery can stimulate spontaneous meditation.*
"Hallelujah! I will praise the LORD with all my heart in the assembly of the upright and in the congregation. *The LORD's works are great, studied by all who delight in them.* All that he does is splendid and majestic; his righteousness endures forever." - Psalm 111:1-3 CSB
Psalm 145:5

• *Music can help. When King Jehoshaphat asked Elisha to tell him the will of God, Elisha prayed with music in the background.*
"But Jehoshaphat said, "Isn't there a prophet of the LORD here? Let's inquire of the LORD through him." One of the servants of the king of Israel answered, "Elisha son of Shaphat, who used to pour water on Elijah's hands, is here." Jehoshaphat affirmed, "The

word of the LORD is with him." So the king of Israel and Jehoshaphat and the king of Edom went to him. ..."*Now, bring me a musician." While the musician played, the LORD's hand came on Elisha.*" - 2 Kings 3:11-12, 15 CSB

Psalm 42:8

• *Visit a chapel, church, or cathedral.*

"God, you are my God; I eagerly seek you. I thirst for you; my body faints for you in a land that is dry, desolate, and without water. So I gaze on you in the sanctuary to see your strength and your glory. My lips will glorify you because your faithful love is better than life. So I will bless you as long as I live; at your name, I will lift up my hands. You satisfy me as with rich food; my mouth will praise you with joyful lips." - Psalm 63:1-5 CSB"

• *Pray and meditate on God if you cannot sleep.*

"When I think of you as I lie on my bed, *I meditate on you during the night watches* because you are my helper; I will rejoice in the shadow of your wings. I follow close to you; your right hand holds on to me." - Psalm 63:6-8 CSB

I am awake through each watch of the night *to meditate on your promise.*" - Psalm 119:148 CSB

• *Use meditation to present our requests to God and consider what He is directing us to do. Mary did this.*

"But Mary was treasuring up all these things in her heart and meditating on them." - Luke 2:19 CSB

• *Meditation can be used to pray for strength. Jesus meditated in the morning. He prayed and communed with His Father before preaching to the people that day.*

"Very early in the morning, while it was still dark, he got up, went out, and made his way to a deserted place; and there he was praying. Simon and his companions searched for him, and when they found him they said, "Everyone is looking for you." And he said to them, "Let's go on to the neighboring villages so that I may preach there too. This is why I have come." - Mark 1:35-38 CSB

Questions:

1. What do you do when you can't sleep?

2. How can music be helpful?

3. How could visiting a chapel or cathedral help you meditate?

Questions with suggested answers:

1. What do you do when you can't sleep?

Answer: Difficulty sleeping goes by the term insomnia. It can be a real problem because if you do not get enough sleep the next day may be difficult. It appears from the verses above that David had trouble sleeping so he decided to meditate on God during that time. We often fail to get back to sleep because of something that is bothering us, or we have a test or a special meeting the next day. This is a great opportunity to turn that problem over to God. Reciting Scripture can help too like Psalm 23.

2. How can music be helpful?

Answer: Music is prominent in the Bible as a method of worship. It can also help us focus on God in meditation. "Now, bring me a musician." While the musician played, the LORD's hand came on Elisha." - 2 Kings 3:15 CSB. These verses about Elisha are interesting as we get the impression that Elisha used or needed music to help him meditate. When he did meditate, he felt the hand of God. In other words, God spoke, influenced, and guided him during this time. Sometimes music prepares mind to accept God's input.

3. How could visiting a chapel or cathedral help you meditate?

Answer: Chapels and cathedrals can be great places to worship. They are usually quiet, reverent, and decorated with artwork that stimulates a high view of God. If you travel to Europe, you can visit many of the beautiful old cathedrals that have impressive artwork and music. They were designed and built when people were not literate so the paintings of the famous scenes of the Bible were used to instruct the people. At St Mary's Hospital in Rochester, MN where I work there is a wonderful chapel attached to the hospital where many staff, patients and families go to pray for their work with the sick. The Sisters of St Mary's who built the chapel along with the hospital in the late 1800s realized the importance of the spiritual aspect of healing alongside great medical skills of the doctors and nurses. When I rotate through the hospital service I stop in the chapel in the middle of the day. It is quiet, it stills my soul and leads me to meditate and pray for my patients who are suffering. I pray for wisdom in the decisions I have to make with my patients that day.

What are some Bible passages that are useful to meditate on?
• Psalm 8—In this Psalm, David meditates on the awesome nature of God; the order of Creation; the magnificent nature of God. This was pleasing to God.
• Matthew 6:25-34 - In this passage, Jesus tells us how to deal with worry and anxiety. He uses the example of nature and recommends we look to nature to learn how He cares for us. Lastly, He says to just "worry about today" – "one day at a time".
• Matthew 5:13-16 – the end of the Beatitudes. Jesus tells us to be salt and light in the world.

Questions:

1. What happens when you meditate and keep Christ close to your heart?

2. How can meditation help us be "salt and light"?

Questions with suggested answers:

1. What happens when you meditate and keep Christ close to your heart?

Answer: Read this passage to get your answers. "For this reason I kneel before the Father from whom every family in heaven and on earth is named. I pray that he may grant you, according to the riches of his glory, to be strengthened with power in your inner being through his Spirit, and that Christ may dwell in your hearts through faith. I pray that you, being rooted and firmly established in love, may be able to comprehend with all the saints what is the length and width, height and depth of God's love, and to know Christ's love that surpasses knowledge, so that you may be filled with all the fullness of God. Now to him who is able to do above and beyond all that we ask or think according to the power that works in us – to him be glory in the church and in Christ Jesus to all generations, forever and ever. Amen." – Ephesians 3:14-21 CSB

Notice the key things that happen when you meditate on Jesus in prayer:

A) We realize and acknowledge the richness and strength of God; B) He will strengthen your soul – your inner being through the Holy Spirit (not some energy drink); C) You strengthen your spiritual roots; D) You gain spiritual perspective which will affect your world view and the things that are happening to you; E) You realize the love of Jesus and its massive scope to all humankind; F) You refocus on what you can do to give God the glory rather than praying for yourself.

2. How can meditation help us be "salt and light"?

Answer: Jesus' words at the end of the Beatitudes (Matt 5:3-12) are really important to living our lives for Christ and producing glory for God. The function of salt is to prevent decay in foods and to provide flavor. When we are "salt" our lives are different than others. We exemplify the Beatitudes as only a Christian can. We show our light in our behavior. Being "salt and light" requires a daily supply of strength from God. You get that through reading His Word and prayer. Then go out and "shine" and glorify God.

8

Why Should I Go to Church?

What does the Bible say about church? The church is where we go to learn about God and receive instruction from the Bible (word of the LORD). We learn how to "walk with God" and fellowship with other Christians."and many peoples will come and say, "Come, let us go up to the mountain of the LORD, to the house of the God of Jacob. *He will teach us about his ways so that we may walk in his paths*." For instruction will go out of Zion and the word of the LORD from Jerusalem." – Isaiah 2:3 CSB

Who is the Leader of the Church?

• *Jesus – it is His Church.*
"He exercised this power in Christ by raising him from the dead and seating him at his right hand in the heavens – far above every ruler and authority, power and dominion, and every title given, not only in this age but also in the one to come. And he subjected everything under his feet and appointed him as *head over everything for the church, which is his body, the fullness of the one who fills all things in every way*." – Ephesians 1:20-23 CSB

• *Jesus started the church – the collection of all believers from all places and all time.*
Christ died to save us from our sin, to be the sacrifice for us so that we may be righteous in God's sight and spend eternity in heaven. The Church is the bride, and we submit to Jesus as the bridegroom. The Bible uses the marriage metaphor to describe the intimate relationship of Jesus (bridegroom) to the Church (bride). When you go to church you are with people you will spend eternity with!

"because the husband is the head of the wife as *Christ is the head of the church*. He is the Savior of the body. Now as the *church submits to Christ*, so also wives are to submit to their husbands in everything. Husbands, love your wives, just as *Christ loved the church* and ga*ve himself for her to make her holy*, cleansing her with the washing of water by the word. He did this to present the church to himself in splendor, without spot or wrinkle or anything like that, but holy and blameless." – Ephesians 5:23-27 CSB

• *Jesus cares about the Church.*
"For no one ever hates his own flesh but provides and cares for it, *just as Christ does for the church, since we are members of his body.*" – Ephesians 5:29-30 CSB

What is the Church to do?

• *Jesus gave the instructions to us in Matthew 28.* The Church begins after the resurrection of Jesus when He tells His disciples what they are to do. This event was just prior to His ascension into Heaven. The Church is to make disciples (evangelize); baptize; and teach. Jesus also mentions that "He will be there" with us when we do these things.

"Jesus came near and said to them, "All authority has been given to me in heaven and on earth."*Go, therefore, and make disciples of all nations, baptizing them in the name of the Father and of the Son and of the Holy Spirit, "teaching them to observe everything I have commanded you.* And remember, I am with you always, to the end of the age." – Matthew 28:18-20 CSB.

• *Teaching (Mt 28:20), fellowship, communion, prayer, and baptizing new believers.* Preaching and teaching by the Apostles led to conviction of sin, repentance, then baptism, then adding to the membership of the Church. The verses below from Acts 2 are at the end of Peter's sermon. The results were 'church growth'.

"When they heard this, they were pierced to the heart and said to Peter and the rest of the apostles: *"Brothers, what should we do?* "Peter replied, "Repent and be baptized, each of you, in the name of Jesus Christ for the forgiveness of your sins, and you will receive the gift of the Holy Spirit. "For the promise is for you and for your children, and for all who are far off, as many as the Lord our God will call." With many other words he testified and strongly urged them, saying, "Be saved from this corrupt generation! *" So those who accepted his message were baptized, and that day about three thousand people were added to them.*" – Acts 2:37-41 CSB

"They devoted themselves to the apostles' teaching, to the fellowship, to the breaking of bread, and to prayer." – Acts 2:42 CSB
Acts 2:46-47

• Paul said read the Bible, pray, preach, and teach. Exhort is to strongly encourage.
"Command and *teach* these things. Don't let anyone despise your youth, but set an example for the believers in speech, in conduct, in love, in faith, and in purity. *Until I come, give your attention to public reading, exhortation, and teaching.*" – 1 Timothy 4:11-13 CSB

• Praying as a group. The church prays for those in need. Praying together builds unity. Notice this was a mixed prayer meeting – men and women. These group prayers are called 'corporate prayers' where we pray with the church or our small group.
"Then they returned to Jerusalem from the Mount of Olives, which is near Jerusalem – a Sabbath day's journey away. When they arrived, they went to the room upstairs where they were staying: Peter, John, James, Andrew, Philip, Thomas, Bartholomew, Matthew, James the son of Alphaeus, Simon the Zealot, and Judas the son of James. They all were *continually united in prayer*, along with the women, including Mary the mother of Jesus, and his brothers." – Acts 1:12-14 CSB

"When they heard the report, *all the believers lifted their voices together in prayer to God*: "O Sovereign Lord, Creator of heaven and earth, the sea, and everything in them–" – Acts 4:24 NLT

"So Peter was kept in prison, *but the church was praying fervently to God for him.*" – Acts 12:5 CSB

• Education- the apostles taught and developed the church members. The teaching was to be motivated by agape love. This is not a short-term process – Paul did this for a year, and it was a large-group teaching session.
"Then he went to Tarsus to search for Saul, and when he found him he brought him to Antioch. *For a whole year they met with the church and taught large numbers*. The disciples were first called Christians at Antioch." – Acts 11:25-26 CSB

"Now the *goal of our instruction is love* that comes from a pure heart, a good conscience, and a sincere faith." – 1 Timothy 1:5 CSB

• Identify members for specific tasks as guided by the Holy Spirit. This is the idea of being "called to a specific task in the Church". This could be a position in the church or a cross-cultural missionary. Notice that the "they" in this verse were the "church in

Antioch". Ideally, the Church under the direction of the Holy Spirit should call missionaries.
Revelation 3:6 , Acts 13:2

"Then the *apostles and the elders, with the whole church, decided to select men* who were among them and to send them to Antioch with Paul and Barnabas: Judas, called Barsabbas, and Silas, both leading men among the brothers." – Acts 15:22 CSB

• *Outreach -the Church is to go to unreached peoples – wherever they may be. This is the basis of "outreach" where we reach "out beyond the walls of the Church". We do not try to duplicate what others are doing.*
"My aim is to *preach the gospel where Christ has not been named*, so that I will not build on someone else's foundation, but, as it is written, Those who were not told about him will see, and those who have not heard will understand." – Romans 15:20-21 CSB

• *Encourage; appoint leaders (elders) prayer and fasting. The Church chose its leaders not the Roman government. Hardship is part of the deal.*
"After they had *preached the gospel in that town and made many disciples*, they returned to Lystra, to Iconium, and to Antioch, strengthening the disciples by *encouraging* them to continue in the faith and by telling them, "It is *necessary to go through many hardships* to enter the kingdom of God." When they had appointed elders for them in every church and prayed with fasting, they committed them to the Lord in whom they had believed." – Acts 14:21-23 CSB

Acts 1:21-26 CSB

• *Delegate – everyone has a task; no one does everything. The disciples learned early on to delegate. This prevented burnout and also enabled many to get involved. As the saying goes, "many hands make light work."*
"The Twelve summoned the whole company of the disciples and said, "*It would not be right for us to give up preaching the word of God to wait on tables.* Brothers and sisters, select from among you seven men of good reputation, full of the Spirit and wisdom, whom we can appoint to this duty. But we will devote ourselves to prayer and to the ministry of the word." – Acts 6:2-4 CSB

• *Fellowship – the local Church is where we gather to encourage and build each other up. We share our faith stories, joys, and problems. If you do not go to Church, you miss out.*

"*not neglecting to gather together*, as some are in the habit of doing, but *encouraging each other,* and all the more as you see the day approaching." – Hebrews 10:25 CSB

"So then, let us pursue what promotes peace and what *builds up one another.*" – Romans 14:19 CSB

"For I want very much to see you, so that I may impart to you some spiritual gift to strengthen you, that is, *to be mutually encouraged by each other's faith, both yours and mine.*" – Romans 1:11-12 CSB

• *Jesus prayed for unity; He did not pray for uniformity. There is a difference. The goal is "no division in the Church".*

"I pray not only for these, but also for those who believe in me through their word."*May they all be one, as you, Father, are in me and I am in you.* May they also be in us, so that the world may believe you sent me." – John 17:20-21 CSB
1 Corinthians 12:24-26

• *Church size is not detailed. Some churches start small, some stay small some get big. The mission remains the same.*

"Also give my greetings to the *church that meets in their home.* Greet my dear friend Epenetus. He was the first person from the province of Asia to become a follower of Christ." – Romans 16:5 NLT

"to Apphia our sister, to Archippus our fellow soldier, and to the *church that meets in your home.*" – Philemon 1:2 CSB

• *One church helps another. Churches need to help each other rather than fight and compete with each other.*
Romans 15:25-28 CSB

The Church is the place where people use their spiritual gifts.

• *The Church is made up of saints who serve and are of benefit to others less fortunate. Phoebe was singled out by Paul as being particularly noteworthy. Her ministry was to all believers. Paul said, "she helped me too."*

"I commend to you our sister Phoebe, who is a servant of the church in Cenchreae. So you should welcome her in the Lord in a manner worthy of the saints and assist her in whatever matter she may require your help. For indeed she has been a *benefactor of many – and of me also.*" – Romans 16:1-2 CSB

• *The Church was composed of people with differing strengths and gifts.*

"Now in the church at Antioch *there were prophets and teachers*: Barnabas, Simeon who was called Niger, Lucius of Cyrene, Manaen, a close friend of Herod the tetrarch, and Saul." – Acts 13:1 CSB

• *The church is where we exercise our spiritual gift. It takes all of us with our variety of gifts to make a local church body effective. "One body, many parts".*

1 Corinthians 12:12-31 CSB

"Now as we have many parts in one body, and all the parts do not have the same function, in the same way we who are many are *one body in Christ and individually members of one another.*" – Romans 12:4-5 CSB

• *The Church is a "whole body" – that's every type of person.* Who are these people in your church? The purpose of these gifts is to "build up the Church" so that it attains unity in the faith. Unity and maturity, not uniformity – these are the characteristics important to Church life.

Ephesians 4:11-16

What happens in church?

• *Spiritual instruction. Members who are gifted in teaching use that spiritual gift.*

"Then he went to Tarsus to search for Saul, and when he found him he brought him to Antioch. *For a whole year they met with the church and taught large numbers.* The disciples were first called Christians at Antioch." – Acts 11:25-26 CSB

• *Singing and music and teaching- all of this should be constructive and building up of people.*

"What then, brothers and sisters? Whenever you come together, each one has a hymn, a teaching, a revelation, another tongue, or an interpretation. Everything is to be done for building up." – 1 Corinthians 14:26 CSB

• *Prayer for the sick.*

"Is anyone among you sick? He should call for the elders of the church, and they are to pray over him, anointing him with oil in the name of the Lord. The prayer of faith will save the sick person, and the Lord will raise him up; if he has committed sins, he will be forgiven." – James 5:14-15 CSB

When should we go to Church? The Old Testament Sabbath is Saturday. The Apostles met on Sunday (the first day of the week). There is no rigid commandment. Jesus was resurrected on Sunday hence most church services are Saturday night or Sunday.

"*On the first day of the week*, we assembled to break bread. Paul spoke to them, and since he was about to depart the next day, he kept on talking until midnight." – Acts 20:7 CSB

How shall the Church be run? We learn church management principles from some of the books in the New Testament of the Bible. These were actually letters written to specific Churches. For example, "Paul, Silvanus, and Timothy: To the church of the Thessalonians in God the Father and the Lord Jesus Christ. Grace to you and peace." – 1 Thessalonians 1:1 CSB

• *The church building itself can be anywhere and does not have to be an expensive, ornate building. They can meet in your house. House churches were common in Bible times and are found today in many places.*

"Paul, a prisoner of Christ Jesus, and Timothy our brother: To Philemon our dear friend and coworker, to Apphia our sister, to Archippus our fellow soldier, *and to the church that meets in your home.*" – Philemon 1:1-2 CSB

• *Church buildings are temporary and earthly. They are simply part of the need to fulfill the Mission. John writes in Revelation that he saw no church buildings in Heaven.*

"I did not see a temple in it, because the Lord God the Almighty and the Lamb are its temple." – Revelation *21:22 CSB*

• *Services should be orderly. Paul says this writing to the Corinthian church.*
"But everything is to be done *decently and in order.*" – 1 Corinthians 14:40 CSB

• *The Church is to be a place to bring tithes and offerings so it can fulfill the mission. The Church gets "reward points" for faithful giving.*
"Bring the full tenth into the storehouse so that there may be food in my house. Test me in this way, says the LORD of Armies. See if I will not open the floodgates of heaven and pour out a blessing for you without measure." – Malachi 3:10 CSB
Philippians 4:15-17

• *The Church is to be discerning and focused on the people it helps.*
"If any believing woman has widows in her family, let her help them. Let the church not be burdened, so that it *can help widows in genuine need.*" – 1 Timothy 5:16 CSB

How does the Church deal with complaints and disagreements? What issues can interfere with the mission of the Church?

• *As the Church grows there will be complaints.*
"In those days, as the disciples were increasing in number, there *arose a complaint by the Hellenistic Jews against the Hebraic Jews* that their widows were being overlooked in the daily distribution." – Acts 6:1 CSB

• *There will be disagreements. At times churches may "agree to disagree" and go separate ways.*
"Barnabas wanted to take along John Mark. But Paul insisted that they should not take along this man who had deserted them in Pamphylia and had not gone on with them to the work. They had such a sharp disagreement that they parted company, and Barnabas took Mark with him and sailed off to Cyprus. But Paul chose Silas and departed, after being commended by the brothers and sisters to the grace of the Lord." – Acts 15:37-40 CSB

• *Even missionaries will disagree. Why? Because they are people and people have disagreements. These disagreements are disruptive and can hurt the mission.*
"I urge Euodia and I urge Syntyche to agree in the Lord. Yes, I also ask you, true partner, to help these women who have contended for the gospel at my side, along with Clement and the rest of my coworkers whose names are in the book of life." – Philippians 4:2-3 CS
Galatians 5:15

• *The Church is to avoid "foolish debates". Make sure that what you are debating is really essential and worthy of debate.*

"But *avoid foolish debates*, genealogies, quarrels, and disputes about the law, because they are unprofitable and worthless." – Titus 3:9 CSB

• *The Church is to have discernment. There may be false believers that creep in. How do we discern who the real believers are?*

"They went out from us, *but they did not belong to us; for if they had belonged to us, they would have remained with us*. However, they went out so that it might be made clear that none of them belongs to us." – 1 John 2:19 CSB

Acts 20:28-30

• *Church discipline. The Church is the place to settle sinful but non-criminal situations between believers. The Church does not deal with issues that concern non-believers.*

"If your brother sins against you, go and rebuke him in private. If he listens to you, you have won your brother. "But if he won't listen, take one or two others with you, so that by the testimony of two or three witnesses every fact may be established. If he doesn't pay attention to them, tell the church. If he doesn't pay attention even to the church, let him be like a Gentile and a tax collector to you." – Matthew 18:15-17 CSB

Questions:

1. Should I become a member of a local church? Why can't I just attend?

2. Why can't I just watch online?

3. How do I find a church in my town? What if I am on a business trip or vacation, how do I find a place to worship?

4. Do I need to give money to the church I go to? What if I am really poor right now?

Questions with suggested answers:

1. Should I become a member of a local church? Why can't I just attend?

Answer: Most churches are open to anyone to come into a service – certainly that is the case for most evangelical churches that are trying to fulfill the Great Commission of Matthew 28. If you are living long-term in a community and attend a local church eventually you should consider becoming a member. Membership is for those who have become Christ followers and have repented of their sins and are living their life for Jesus. Many times, a newly converted person will be baptized and become a member of the local church at the same time. However, since many of us move with our jobs it is likely at some point in your life that you will leave one church and join another. This does not require baptism again, but it will typically require you to meet with the pastor and church elders to give your testimony – the story behind how you came to be a follower of Jesus Christ. This ensures that the members of the local church are true believers (as best one can tell), are living their life according to the Scriptures, and agree with the Church statement of faith. As mentioned above, the church members need to be unified in what they believe but not uniform in style of worship, dress, gifts etc.

Being a member of a local church will give you a sense of ownership, will enable you to vote and participate in decisions, and enable you to serve in that church in key areas. Since all of us are given spiritual gifts, it is important that you use them and ideally you do that in person with others. There are many ways to serve from working with children, to ushering, leading a Bible study, or going on mission trips. In some churches you will not need to be a member to serve in some of these areas but typically when it comes to teaching or preaching membership will be required. The reason for this is membership requires you to agree to the statement of faith. This protects the local church from false teachers. A church that believes in the Bible will never give its pulpit to someone who is an unbeliever or a person who claims to be a believer but is preaching false doctrine.

2. Why can't I just watch online?

Answer: You can and sometimes it is necessary. During the pandemic of 2020-2023 we learned how to livestream our services. People got used to getting up 5 minutes before the service and watching it during breakfast and then going out to enjoy the rest of the day. Some people as of 2024 are still doing church this way and there may be good medical reasons for that depending on your health and the level of virus in your area. Watching online is also really effective for people who have to work on Sunday, such as those in the medical profession. In general, however you will get more out of worship and serve the Church by being there in person. That was the way the Church of Acts did it. It's hard to have fellowship when you are watching online. It is also impossible to have a children's ministry without kids to minister to!

3. How do I find a church in my town? What if I am on a business trip or vacation, how do I find a place to worship?

Answer: If you are already a member of a denomination then one obvious way is to look up a church of that group that is near you and check it out. Of course, you can ask around and get people's recommendation. Another way that works is to simply Google "evangelical churches near me" then go to the website of that church and most of the time you will find their "statement of faith". Sometimes this is entitled, "what we believe". Then read it and see if it Bible-based. A good quite detailed one is found on the website of The Moody Church in Chicago (https://www.moodychurch.org/what-we-believe/#1508360857097-70e8cfd3-8ae1). Then of course visit several churches and see where God is leading you.

4. Do I need to give money to the church I go to? What if I am really poor right now?

Answer: What you give to God is in proportion to what you earn. Jesus illustrated this in the story of the widow's mite. "Sitting across from the temple treasury, he watched how the crowd dropped money into the treasury. Many rich people were putting in large sums. Then a poor widow came and dropped in two tiny coins worth very little. Summoning his disciples, he said to them, "Truly I tell you, this poor widow has put more into the treasury than all the others. For they all gave out of their surplus, but she out of her poverty has put in everything she had -- all she had to live on." - Mark 12:41-44 CSB. Most people give less than 5% of their income to charitable causes. This falls short of the 10% (tithe) that is recommended in the Old Testament. If you do not have a lot of money you can give in different ways. Giving of your time to help out the local church or give produce grown in your garden or farm are also ways to give back. Sometimes we are tempted to wait to start giving until we have more money. It is better to give regularly as you go through life. In 2022, many people saw their retirement funds that they had been saving for many years plummet in value by 25% as the stock market dropped. By giving over the years (rather than saving it all) the money would have been effective at reducing suffering. Always remember – giving should be proportional to your income. If you are making $40,000/year and give $4000 (10%) to charity you are giving more in God's eyes than the billionaire who gives $10,000 (1%). People may think – "Wow, $10,000" but actually the $4000 gift is more generous gift in God's eyes. That is the point of the story of the "widow's mite" in Mark 12. Read it again.

Thomas Witzig

Epilogue

Now that you have finished the book look at **Figure 4** – have you grown spiritually? For sure you are physically older now, but are you also more mature spiritually? I trust that the Word of God has and is working in your life. If you continue to read His Word and follow it, you will make progress in your spiritual life up until you take your last deep breath on this earth and move to eternity to be with Jesus. I look forward to seeing you there! Remember when you close your eyes in death you will go through your eternal passport control. The example of "your spiritual passport" (**Figure 5** on page 155) is a reminder that entry to Heaven is based on your personal decision to accept Jesus' sacrifice for your sins.

Figure 4: Mark your physical and spiritual ages now and aim to continue to grow spiritually.

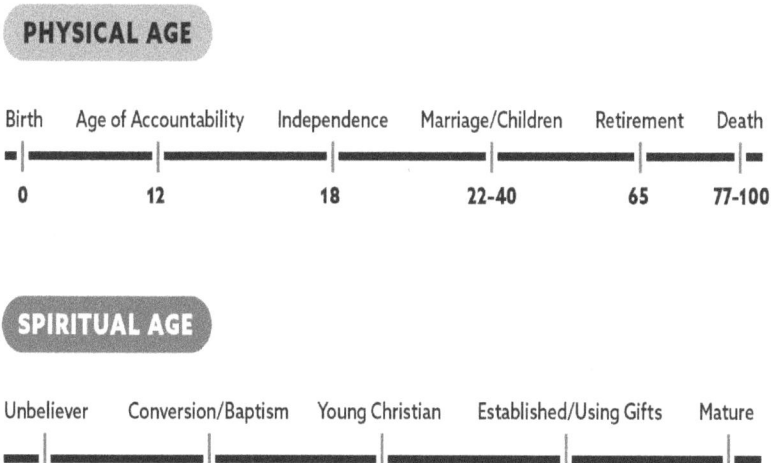

PHYSICAL AGE

Birth	Age of Accountability	Independence	Marriage/Children	Retirement	Death
0	12	18	22-40	65	77-100

SPIRITUAL AGE

Unbeliever Conversion/Baptism Young Christian Established/Using Gifts Mature

Thomas Witzig

Appendix

How to become a Christ follower.

1. Admit we have a problem. We have a sin nature; we were born with it.

We all have at some time in our life committed a sin or sinned in general and thus have fallen short (missed the mark) of perfection.

"For all have sinned and fall short of the glory of God." - Romans 3:23 CSB

2. God requires a sacrifice for our sin, and it is Jesus. Each person must deal with the sin problem in their own lives. Entrance to Heaven requires us to be sinless (like Jesus) *or* have a sacrifice for the sin that we committed. Why? Very early in world history Adam and Eve sinned (Genesis 3) and God required an animal to be sacrificed to provide a covering for that sin. This was the beginning of blood sacrifice for sin. In the Old Testament this was the blood of an animal. God clearly showed us the need for blood in the story of Cain and Abel in Genesis 4. God did not accept Cain's sacrifice of vegetables but did accept Abel's sacrifice of blood. Why? We are not told – it's just the way God set it up. God wants us to go to Heaven, so He made it straightforward. Jesus (God the Son) has always existed with God and the Holy Spirit in Heaven. To be the ultimate blood sacrifice, Jesus was sent in the form of a human being to earth for 33 years. By living a sinless life, when He was crucified, His shed blood fulfilled the need for a blood sacrifice for sin and appeased once for all the sin of all humans. There was an additional requirement - each person needs to *believe in and trust* in the blood sacrifice of Jesus as their *personal Savior* from eternal punishment. This is similar to the Old Testament when people *individually* had to bring the sacrificial animal to the Temple. Or in the case of the Israelites in Egypt they had to apply the blood of the animal on the doorpost of the house to avoid death of the firstborn. Each father had to do it –one household could not do it for the neighborhood. Thus, Jesus sacrificial death was for all people; however, all individually need to accept the gift. Since all of us have committed sin, we need to repent of that sin, accept Christ's sacrifice, and have the righteousness of God credited to our account so that we are considered "right in His sight". This is summarized in Paul's message to the Philippians "... I no longer count on my own righteousness through obeying the law; rather, I become righteous through faith in Christ. For God's way of making us right with himself depends on faith." - Philippians 3:9 NLT or as the CSB says "… not having a righteousness of my own from the law, but one that is through faith in Christ -- *the righteousness from God based on faith*." - Philippians 3:9 CSB

3. Is there really an afterlife? The Bible says that there is eternity waiting for us after we die. At some point after we die, we are individually judged.

"For it is written, As I live, says the Lord, every knee will bow to me, and every tongue will give praise to God. So then, *each of us will give an account of himself to God*." - Romans 14:11-12 CSB

Hebrews 4:12-13 CSB

Thus, the goal of having our sins forgiven is to spend eternity with God in Heaven rather than eternal separation from Him. In this earthly life things may not go well for us, and we may suffer greatly; but *eternity will be different*. Paul describes this as "our hope". This hope is based on the resurrection of Christ after He was crucified for our sins.

"If in this life only we have hope in Christ, we are of all men most miserable." - 1 Corinthians 15:19 KJV
1 Corinthians 15:20-22

4. We need to *believe* and *trust* that the blood of Christ will get us into eternity and that requires *faith*.

Jesus said, "Don't let your heart be troubled. *Believe in God; believe also in me*." - John 14:1 CSB

Since Jesus is not currently on the earth where we can see or touch Him, we cannot definitively prove that believing on Him and trusting Him will get us into Heaven. So, some people struggle with this, and they try to work their way into Heaven. They keep some sort of mental scorecard or spreadsheet that has a column for good works and one for sins. They try to make sure the good outweighs the bad. God wants us to do good works *after* we believe in the sacrifice of Jesus for our sins. They do count for rewards, but they are not in of themselves sufficient for salvation.

• *Belief and trust must be mixed with faith – enough faith to believe in the unseen Jesus, to believe in the Bible's instructions.*

"After all, is God the God of the Jews only? Isn't he also the God of the Gentiles? Of course he is. There is only one God, and *he makes people right with himself only by faith*, whether they are Jews or Gentiles." - Romans 3:29-30 NLT

"Now *faith is the reality of what is hoped for, the proof of what is not seen.* For by it our ancestors won God's approval. By faith we understand that the universe was created by the word of God, so that what is seen was made from things that are not visible." - Hebrews 11:1-3 CSB.

You may say, "its really tough for me to believe that Jesus can get me into Heaven. That's a big slice of faith." But, when you think about it, you do a lot of things by faith without understanding the mechanism. You trust that when you get out of bed that gravity will keep your feet planted on the floor and you will not float up to the ceiling.

5, Grace, not works. Grace is undeserved. When a student gets an answer partially wrong on a test in school the law would say the student gets no credit. However, if the teacher gives the student grace, they will say, "I see that you understood the concept so I will be graceful and let you take credit." In the spiritual realm, grace is the *underserved gift of God* – undeserved because we are not perfect; a gift because it is given by God and must be received. We need God to be graceful to us."For the wages of sin is death, but the *gift of God* is eternal life in Christ Jesus our Lord." - Romans 6:23 CSB. Good works are not sufficient in and of themselves to get us to heaven because they rely on our own power, and we just do not have enough power to live perfectly. Paul summarizes this in Romans 8 - "*The law of Moses was unable to save us because of the weakness of our sinful nature.* So, God did what the law could not do. He sent his own Son in a body like the bodies we sinners have. And in that body God declared an end to sin's control over us by giving his Son as a sacrifice for our sins. He did this so that the just requirement of the law would be fully satisfied for us, who no longer follow our sinful nature but instead follow the Spirit." - Romans 8:3-4 NLT

6. Surrender. There is a great natural desire to achieve a goal on our own merits. We live in a merit-based society where are told that achievement comes from hard work and discipline. When it comes to spiritual things, indeed discipline and living a good life is very important but it is not sufficient to achieve Heaven because that requires perfection.

So, we must get the order right – trust Christ's sacrifice for our sin, become a Christian *then* the good works that follow are important.

7. Count the cost before committing to Jesus. Like any project or relationship, we enter into there is a cost and we need to be sure before we commit. There is a cost to following Jesus. The main "costs" are that we cannot do whatever we want, and we may be despised by others for our faith. Examine the words of Jesus as recorded Luke -

"If you want to be my disciple, you must hate everyone else by comparison--your father and mother, wife and children, brothers and sisters--yes, even your own life. Otherwise, you cannot be my disciple. And if you do not carry your own cross and follow me, you cannot be my disciple."*But don't begin until you count the cost. For who would begin construction of a building without first calculating the cost to see if there is enough money to finish it?* Otherwise, you might complete only the foundation before running out of money, and then everyone would laugh at you. They would say, 'There's the person who started that building and couldn't afford to finish it!' "Or what king would go to war against another king without first sitting down with his counselors to discuss whether his army of 10,000 could defeat the 20,000 soldiers marching against him? And if he can't, he will send a delegation to discuss terms of peace while the enemy is still far away. So you cannot become my disciple without giving up everything you own." - Luke 14:26-33 NLT

8. He leads we follow. Where to? We follow Him as He leads us through life's experiences to our Heavenly Home.

"Then Jesus said to his disciples, "If anyone wants to follow after me, let him deny himself, take up his cross, and follow me." - Matthew 16:24 CSB

9. Are there other ways to get to Heaven other than through Jesus?
"*There is salvation in no one else*, for there is no other name under heaven given to people by which we must be saved." - Acts 4:12 CSB
Acts 15:11, John 10:1,

"I am the gate. If anyone enters by me, he will be saved and will come in and go out and find pasture." - John 10:9 CSB

"I -- I am the LORD. Besides me, there is no Savior. I alone declared, saved, and proclaimed -- and not some foreign god among you. So you are my witnesses -- this is the LORD's declaration -- and I am God. - Isaiah 43:11-12 CSB

John 3:5 CSB

"I have been the LORD your God ever since the land of Egypt; you know no God but me, and no Savior exists besides me." - Hosea 13:4 CSB

10. Benefit package of being a follower of Jesus.

• *Eternal life is our inheritance after we become a Christ-follower.* Remember, we inherit, not earn, eternal life. Our righteousness comes by faith and is a remarkable gift from God. Our sins are erased because of Jesus, not because of a pile of good works. Our account with God is credited with Christ's righteousness and we are now able to inherit eternal life.

"Your reward for trusting him will be the salvation of your souls." 1 Peter 1:9, NLT.

"He declared us not guilty because of his great kindness. And now we know that we will inherit eternal life." Titus 3:7, NLT.

Philippians 3:9 CSB

• *We are no longer a slave to sin. We now have an eternal inheritance.*
"And because you are sons, God sent the Spirit of his Son into our hearts, crying, "Abba, Father! " So you are *no longer a slave but a son*, and if a son, then God has made you an heir." - Galatians 4:6-7 CSB

• *Death has been conquered (destroyed; abolished); we no longer fear death.*
"This has now been made evident through the appearing of our Savior Christ Jesus, who has *abolished death and has brought life and immortality to light through the gospel*." - 2 Timothy 1:10 CSB

• *We are made "right in His sight". Claiming the sacrifice of Jesus as the bearer of our sin makes us appear perfect in God's sight.*
"And he is entirely fair and just in this present time when he declares sinners to be right in his sight because they believe in Jesus." Romans 3:26, NLT.

• *We get a fresh start, so look forward not backward.*
"Therefore, if anyone is in Christ, *he is a new creation*; the old has passed away, and see, the new has come!" - 2 Corinthians 5:17 CSB

• *We are justified. Justification is a one-time judicial act where God applies credit from Jesus. We then appear "just as if we never sinned". This is a free gift but not cheap— it cost Jesus much suffering and death.*
"They are justified freely by his grace through the redemption that is in Christ Jesus." - Romans 3:24 CSB

• *We have peace with God.*
"Therefore, since we have been declared righteous by faith, *we have peace with God* through our Lord Jesus Christ." - Romans 5:1 CSB

• *We receive the Holy Spirit.* The Holy Spirit is a gift that comes only after conversion. Jesus and the Holy Spirit now help us live a life in accordance to the Scriptures and to do good works. We are justified once but achieving holy living is the ongoing process of sanctification (becoming holy) that is driven by the power of the Holy Spirit.

"Peter replied, "Each of you must turn from your sins and turn to God, and be baptized in the name of Jesus Christ for the forgiveness of your sins. Then you will receive the gift of the Holy Spirit." Acts 2:38, NLT.

In summary, let's put this plan of salvation into the analogy of a passport.

The Spiritual Passport Analogy. When we travel outside of our home country, we need a passport. The passport has our personal information and our photo. It must be up to date and valid. When we enter the new country or return to our home country, we go through a checkpoint called passport control. Each person with passport in hand file one by one to the serious-looking officer in the booth who checks our passport to give permission to enter. They then stamp our passport for approval. When we go through this process, we do it alone; we don't go through with someone else or using someone else's passport. *There is no other way to get into the new country without our individual valid stamped passport.*

Using this analogy, when we come to the Eternal Passport Control after we die there are two lines – one line is labeled "for perfect people" and the other is labeled "for sinners". If you ask the angel controlling the lines, "I was a really good person during my life with few sins, can I go to the 'perfect line'? They will say "No, even one sin makes you a 'sinner' and thus you need to go through the line for sinners. We have never seen a perfect person yet." So, the line for sinners is long but it moves fast.

One woman tries to go to the passport manager with her husband and go in under his passport, but she is sent back and told, "each person must come in on their own account". The passport control manager looks quickly through the pages of each person's passport. The officer is looking for a "blood stamp" a blot of blood that has engraved underneath, "the blood of Jesus Christ shed for you" that makes them perfect in God's sight. People that have the blood stamp pass quickly through the gate and move into a great hall with a large sign over it entitled "Heaven". As the door to the Great Hall opens, we get a glimpse of the large crowd of people who are rejoicing as they meet fellow believers and begin their eternity with Jesus. It looks beautiful and full of light.

A man steps to the line with a very thick passport with many pages. As the officer skims through the pages he comments, "I notice that you have been to many countries and have done many good works –feeding the poor, helping orphans and the sick. But I don't see a 'blood stamp'. Where is it?" The man replies, "well I never thought that I needed the blood stamp since I had so many good works." The manager says, "I'm really sorry but the blood stamp is needed." "Can I go back and get one the man asks?" "No, you have died, and we don't allow people to go back to earth. It's a one-way gate. You will now need to follow the black line to the Hallway marked 'Eternal Punishment'". In that Hallway there is darkness and no light as the people are separated from God. The exact nature of their punishment is not known but it will not be a happy place.

Someday all of us will die and go through Eternal Passport Control. God has made it really easy to have the acceptable passport for Heaven because there is only One Way to get it. He said the requirement is to acknowledge that we have committed sin, trust in the blood sacrifice of Jesus for that sin; be truly sorry for what we did and turn from it to believe that the blood of Jesus will be enough and live our life for Jesus. That process of being genuinely sorry for our sin and being willing to turn from it is called "repentance". Once we have repented and have received the gift of Christ's sacrifice for our sin our eternal passport is stamped with the Blood Stamp. After that life-changing decision we go about living and working for Christ and adding good works to the other pages of the passport. These will determine our eternal rewards once inside Heaven.

Thomas Witzig

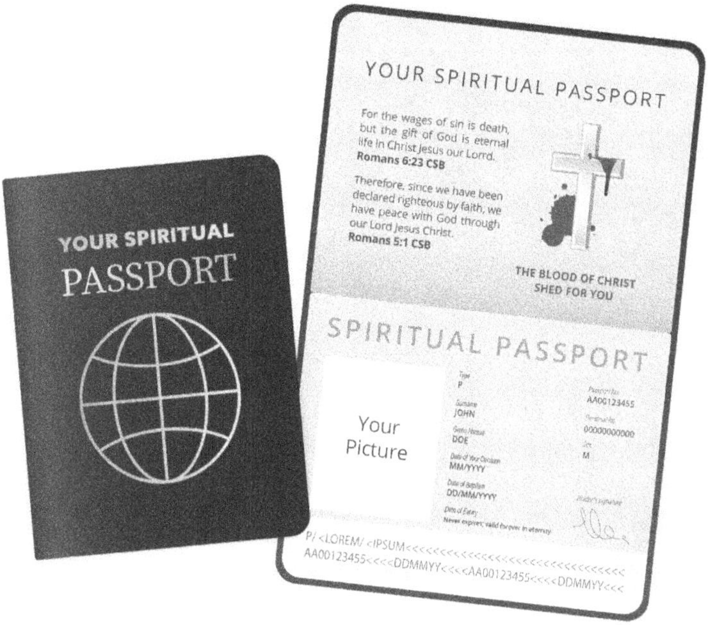

Figure 5: The Spiritual Passport visual is a reminder to you of the reality that there will be a judgement day for each of us after we die. Spending eternity in Heaven requires acceptance of the sacrifice that Jesus made for us when He died and shed His blood as the payment for your sin. He has already done it for you and wants you to accept. Like any gift, it must be opened and accepted by the recipient. Similar to your earthly passport, make sure your "spiritual passport" is signed and stamped so that you are ready for eternity. Do it now!

Other books by Thomas Witzig:

Mostly Scripture Q.D. A Topical Study for Daily Living. Published by BookBaby

www.ingramcontent.com/pod-product-compliance
Lightning Source LLC
Chambersburg PA
CBHW050020100426
42739CB00011B/2721